OUT THE ORGANIZATION:

How Fast Could You Find a New Job?

Madeleine and Robert Swain

MASTER
MEDIA
LIMITED

MASTERMEDIA and colophon are registered trademarks of
MasterMedia Corporation
Designed by Irving Perkins Associates, Inc.
Manufactured in the United States of America

10   9   8   7   6   5   4   3   2

LIBRARY OF CONGRESS CATALOGING IN PUBLICATION DATA

Swain, Madeleine.
   Out the organization.

   Bibliography: p.
   Includes index.
   1. Job hunting.   I. Swain, Robert (Robert L.)
HF5382.7.S92   1988   650.1′4   87-31380

ISBN 0-942361-10-5

OUT THE ORGANIZATION is dedicated to those
who lived this experience with us, including
Alex, Anne, Barbara, Barry, Bill, Bob, Carol,
Caroline, David, Dawn, Deborah, Deryck, Don,
Ed, Ellen, Eric, Ernie, Evan, Frank, Fred,
George, Hans, Jeanette, Jim, John, Keith, Ken,
L.C., Leonard, Linda, Lisa, Lou, Louie, Lyman,
Marge, Marty, Marylou, Michael, Myron, Nancy,
Naomi, Nigel, Pat, Paul, Peg, Perry, Peter, Ron,
Ruth, Steve, Susan, Suzanne, Ted, Tim, Tip, Todd,
Tom, Walter, and others.

Contents

Acknowledgments

We want to further acknowledge several people who have made significant contributions to this book:

Bill Stewart and Linda Mead for providing us with much of the theoretical basis for developing a state of the art outplacement practice;

Beth Greenfeld for her excellent and thorough research and contributions to the structure of our manuscript;

Susan Stautberg, our publisher, for the encouragement to begin and complete this book.

MADELEINE & ROBERT SWAIN

Foreword

Neurotic (adj.)—when you worry about things that didn't happen in the past, instead of worrying about something that won't happen in the future, like normal people.—[anon.]

W E understand the feelings that accompany trouble on the job—the uncertainty, anxiety, worries about the future. And we know what it's like to be fired—we have both been through it.

Some of our experiences from those troubled times are indelibly etched in our memories. We each knew doubt about getting the next job; concern about dwindling resources; discomfort at standing in an unemployment line; bruised egos and loss of self-esteem—and a dread of meeting new people socially and having to answer that standard conversation-opener: "And what do you do?"

But we each survived our individual setbacks, and in time—with experience gained in careers in marketing and consulting—we felt that we wanted to work with the increasing flow of displaced executives and middle managers by offering counsel to the organizations that were terminating these individuals.

So, about ten years ago, Swain & Swain hung out a shingle in New York's Chrysler Building, and a new corporate outplacement consulting firm was born.

For those of you readers not familiar with outplacement, we suggest a simple definition for what is a relatively new industry: "Outplacement is a service offered by corporations to their employees in order to help them find new employment. The services provided by outplacement firms include: advice and counsel on how to develop appropriate strategies and tactics for a job search or a new career; help in 'positioning' oneself for whatever markets and audiences are going to be targeted; interview training and management; psychological testing and assessment; and full support and professional guidance during the entire process."

As Swain & Swain grew, and we gained in expertise, confidence, and clientele, we witnessed more than the normal changes that time brings to any institution in society—we saw the beginnings of the transformation of American businesses and institutions. Some of the most significant changes have been:

- The steady and dramatic erosion of the middle management section of the corporate pyramid, and the concomitant loss of managerial jobs.

- The record number of women joining the workforce; their both moving up and falling off the corporate ladder.

- The increase in people starting their own businesses—some by choice, some by default.

- The unprecedented numbers of organizations enduring streamlining, reorganization, and downsizing—affecting every level and every function.

- The decline of corporate loyalty.

- The erosion of an employee's confidence in job stability.

The result is that it sometimes seems as if the entire workforce is:

- Just out of a job.

- About to be out of a job.

- Dissatisfied with the jobs they have.

- Confused about what to do next.

The services of Swain & Swain are contracted for by corporations and institutions—we are not able to work with individuals without such sponsorship. Our purpose in writing this book is to make available to everyone the career advice and counsel that we usually dispense only to those who have been offered outplacement counseling by their former employers.

We do have a message—and a mission. We want to relieve some of the job seeker's anxiety, and replace it with realistic, practical advice—the sort we supply for a living—to those not fortunate enough to have access to personalized outplacement services.

We want you to realize that you, the individual, have far more control over your destiny than you realize. We know that it is never pleasant to be told that you are superfluous. It is also far from rewarding to catch the 7:18 to the city en route to a less than fulfilling job, and it is certainly anxiety producing to be employed by an about-to-be-merged company in which the certainty of job security has vanished.

We hope that this book will coax you into thinking: thinking about yourself—what has made you feel happy and productive; what has left you feeling isolated and frustrated; what has represented a growth experience that caused you to stretch and rise to the challenge; what and who you are at this stage in your life. Because, ultimately, a "good" job or an "interesting" career is only one that gives you personal satisfaction—one that leaves you fulfilled at the end of your workday.

In arranging our chapters we've included a number of scenarios that deal with various stages and phases of change—changes in job, industry, maybe expectations as well. We've also included a chapter on an issue that has become important in today's work world—what self-employment is about in the late eighties and nineties, as it bridges the gap between corporate experience and entrepreneurial goals.

We also thought a lot about the emotional issues. Some of us are better than others at discussing what bothers us—some of us aren't even sure about the sources of our discomfort or depression. Some of us are deniers, some of us tend toward debilitating anxiety when things go wrong. But some of us adopt a mature, pragmatic attitude toward a troublesome subject and want to know how to make something gone awry better—in short, how to take control. We would like you to gain the competitive edge by learning to take control of your future.

The plain fact is that there are many opportunities today for positive change in one's career—more than ever before existed. While it is true that the job security of yore has gone, the positive side of that development is another dimension of opportunity that had not existed during the days of more "traditional" employment.

Today's job seeker has options in abundance—assuming, of course, that the mindset is open to exploration, creative thinking, and flexibility. Some of the happiest stories from those we have worked with are the less than traditional "success" stories of people who broke out of their prescribed "scripts" and moved into new arenas and levels of personal satisfaction they never would have dreamed possible.

Our success rate—which we measure by how well our clients have done—has been excellent. It should be reassuring to note that 86 percent have gone on to positions and opportunities as good as or better than what they had had before.

Surviving and prospering from "failure" or "discontent" with one's livelihood is what our book is all about. It is really dedicated to all of you who have ever yearned for something better, knowing that it existed, somewhere, but not knowing where or how to begin in its pursuit.

Mounting a job search is very much like many other projects we undertake in our life. There is a definite beginning, middle, and end. Like building a house, it requires a vision, a set of plans, a strong foundation, a person dedicated to overseeing its completion—with attention to quality and follow-through—and a self-sustained, self-initiated effort to see it to fruition.

And, like building a house, there undoubtedly will be "rainy days" when work may appear to be on hold, and possibly times when a few glitches seem momentarily to threaten achieving the desired goals, but the vision must remain.

A well-known outplacement practitioner from the Career Development Team in New York City has been quoted as saying: "When an [unemployed] person wakes up in the morning, looks in the mirror and says, 'I'm an unemployed [worker],' he can't move. When he learns to say, 'I'm a human being with options,' he sees opportunity instead of a dead end."

As in most of life, perception provides the key to our own survival. The old barometer of the half-empty, half-full glass still serves us well. If you're currently seeing it as half empty, look again. It's never too late to try positive thinking.

Today's business marketplace may have fewer chairs at the corporate table—but look around you at the entire banquet hall. There are opportunities for consultancies, joint ventures, franchises, small family businesses, midpreneurial and entrepreneurial projects, and various combinations thereof.

If you doubt that enforced negative circumstances can result in positive opportunity, read on and find out more about change and you. And join us in exploring how you can take control over your career now and become the kind of person you've always wanted to become. As the old adage goes: "If you do what you've always done, you'll get what you always got."

We think you deserve and want more. We hope our book will help guide you through this new journey—think of it as a Baedeker for your campaign. And keep in mind, winners weren't born winners—they learned what worked for them. Unlike a project to build a dream house, your house requires only the tools that you already carry around with you. Perhaps you can hone them on *Out the Organization.*

MADELEINE AND BOB SWAIN

OUT THE
ORGANIZATION

Chapter I
Corporate America Today:
The Changing Pyramid

"The optimist proclaims that we live in the best of all possible worlds; and the pessimist fears this is true."—James Branch Cabell

O**N** May 21, 1987, *The New York Times* ran the following announcement in its business section:

> Dublin, Ohio, May 20 (Reuters)—Wendy's International Inc. said it would eliminate 160 positions, or 20 percent, of its nationwide administrative staff. About half of the cuts will be made at its headquarters here. The company said the action would improve profitability by streamlining its administration and reducing restaurant development expenditures.

If that particular news item had run ten years ago, it would have signaled two important things: (1) trouble for those employees of Wendy's International who were part of the 20 percent to be eliminated and (2) a sign to the financial community that Wendy's might be in difficulty. It would never have occurred to any analyst that Wendy's actions were part of an escalating trend.

But during this decade of the eighties such an event is not only unremarkable, it's what readers of the financial news have come to expect and what employees of America's corporations and institutions have come to know all too well. Wendy's cut-back is simply one more example of change so fundamental to the underpinning of America's business that it is difficult to predict confidently what sort of opportunities will be available to the employee entering the job market of the next decade.

We feel reasonably confident in predicting, however, what sorts of opportunities will *not* be available to these prospective employees. No longer will the potential manager or administrator be able to count on joining an organization—be it for-profit, nonprofit, or government—and expect to spend a lifetime at the same company climbing the corporate or institutional ladder and then retiring on a comfortable pension.

In that dated scenario, the employee rarely worried about job security, and, indeed, unless they committed a truly heinous offense like industrial sabotage or theft of assets, they rarely lost a job unless the company failed.

The roots of corporate life as we know it today are found in the economic environment directly following the second World War. This was a booming, chaotic time as returning servicemen tried to make sense of what they found at home. Their prewar jobs had been usurped by those who had never gone to war; a lot of people had become rich fulfilling war contracts and gained enormous economic clout. Campus culture changed utterly, as the older veterans started classes under the GI Bill—and the women who had been working in factories were expected to return to their domestic tasks and allow the men to take their places on the assembly line. And all those returning men had to find jobs. Some were given their old positions; some were not. Some didn't want them.

William Wyler's 1946 film *The Best Years of Our Lives*, considered today by hard-edged critics to be too sentimental, nevertheless can still bring a tear to the eye as it describes the plight of the returning veteran. The elegant Fredric March, who had been an enlisted man, returns to his job as a bank officer, with a new awareness of the plight of the ordinary guy trying to get ahead.

But it is Dana Andrews, the working-class war hero who comes home a captain, who typifies the dilemma of many. As an officer who had commanded men, the idea of returning to his prewar job of soda jerk is inconceivable. The character played by Andrews is swept about by the vicissitudes of the script, but at the movie's end his energy and maturity, gained at the front, enables him to prevail: he finds the money to start a business; he becomes the new postwar entrepreneur.

By the 1950s, the economic situation had settled down somewhat. For those who were entering the job market, there were certain predictable choices for the white collar worker and others of the educated middle class. For both men and women, there were professions: law; medicine; accounting; government service; communications; retailing or manufacturing; real estate; and, mostly for men, finance and the corporate world. Women were welcome in the latter two only as secretaries and other support staff.

We do not mean to suggest that there have been no dramatic economic changes during the thirty-plus years between the Eisenhower administration and today. There have been recessions and recoveries, two wars—Korea and Vietnam—changes of administrations, fluctuations of interest rates and declining sectors in our economy, like agriculture and heavy industry. The wheel of business trends continues to turn, but until the late seventies one thing had remained reasonably stable: the responsibility felt by corporations and institutions for their employees, which fostered reciprocal loyalty from the employee. Employee and employer have had a relationship of mutuality; each knew what to expect of the other.

It was possible, for instance, for a young man returning from the South Pacific in 1945 who had gotten a job with AT&T in that year still to be employed by the company in 1975. AT&T took care of him, he expected it to and rewarded the company with loyalty and hard work. At retirement, he received his pension and moved to the Sun Belt. That's how things were supposed to work in corporate America.

But during the early eighties, it became clear that the unwritten contract defining mutual responsibility between employer and employee was not holding up so well. First a few—then not so few—long-time employees found themselves being forced into unwanted early retirement; then an increasing number of long-time employees were terminated.

Sources, such as the Bureau of Labor Statistics and *Time* magazine, have estimated variously that between 1983 and 1987 600,000 to 1.2 million managers earning more than $40,000 were fired. And to come? During the next two years, approximately 300,000 more middle- and top-level managers will be looking for work.

These layoffs are the result of nothing less than a complete restructuring of a majority of America's previously stalwart corporations and institutions. We now live in an economic world of the high-tech that enables financial and business institutions to maintain almost constant relationships with other organizations around the world. With the information explosion and new abilities to manage complicated transactions unknown a work generation ago, a plethora of mega- and multi- and omni-organizations has arisen, all of which seek greater profits for their shareholders or greater power for their directors. Their interests and influence cross national boundaries; they are truly international in scope.

If a company is a little corporate fish, or even a middle-sized corporate fish, the chances of it being swallowed up by one of the whales is awfully good. If it's been successful, it could be a profitable addition to someone's stable; if not, an attractive tax write-off. Companies go to extreme lengths to ward off an unfriendly takeover, sometimes incurring enormous debt in the effort. The retrenchment period, even if the attempt has been defeated, may be painful and nonproductive: with no ready cash, staff is laid off; research and development slows; expansion becomes impossible.

But not only a passion for takeover affects today's businesses and institutions. Competitive frenzy and a desire to dominate a share of the marketplace is partner to several other fundamental changes prevalent in the world economy. A special report in the February 16, 1987, issue of *Time* magazine states that "forced upon business by unprecedented global competition and financial turbulence, the change is so swift and powerful that it is churning across the business landscape with the force of an army of bulldozers. American companies have started the huge task of rebuilding themselves from the ground up . . . newly cost-conscious executives are on a relentless examination of the efficiency and effectiveness of everything they do."

Indeed, American businesses must engage in "relentless examination" or they will not find themselves still in business during the 1990s.

During the early 1980s, for example, the Fortune 500 companies saw only a 2 percent increase in sales—and a 17.4 percent decrease in profits. They, and other less illustrious organizations, faced with real competition from abroad, have had to ruthlessly slash staff and costs. Manufacturing overseas has become necessary for many—even an AT&T telephone now may say "Made in China."

With our enormous trade deficit, and financial interest from abroad in purchasing American corporations, as well as active foreign competition, the company or institution that manages to keep its identity will be one that eliminates nonproductive bloat in a struggle to become leaner, more efficient, more able to do battle if necessary.

There is no organization so healthy that it can ignore the newly codified laws of survival. Examples of companies that investigate every financial nook and cranny in their structure are countless. Among them, witness the following representative smattering:

- IBM is reducing its workforce in the United States and has closed three plants.

- The R. J. Reynolds Tobacco Company, in response to increased competition, announced that by the end of 1987 they would offer about 2,800 employees (of a 16,200-member domestic workforce) enhanced pension packages if they would agree to retire.

- Eastman Kodak, traditionally paternalistic, terminated the employment of nearly 13,000 of its 129,000-member workforce.

- The Mellon Bank offered early retirement to 300 senior executives. In 1985, 365 Mellon executives retired under a similar plan of supplementary payments added on to pensions. Mellon in 1987 reported a first-quarter loss of almost $60 million and halved its dividend. In addition, its CEO was dismissed.

- In an effort to bolster the price of their stock, during 1985 and 1986 almost 200 companies repurchased large amounts, among them Philip Morris and Union Carbide.

- General Mills divested itself of its clothing and toy divisions and in so doing wrote off $188 million.

- Restructuring and downsizing obviously results in the dismissal of whole strata of managers: United Airlines in 1987 terminated more than 1,000 employees; CBS and ABC are enduring bloodbaths that have left thousands unemployed; AT&T has eliminated almost 30,000 jobs; General Motors has closed five plants—and for ITT, Xerox, Dow Chemical, Polaroid, Exxon, it's more of the same.

- Then there are the acquisitions—4,000 of them in 1986: General Electric of RCA; Delta Airlines of Western; Capital Cities of ABC; Turner Broadcasting of MGM—as well as all those hundreds of companies that are not household names.

Some parts of the United States are industrialized but nondiversified—these are the company towns. During this decade, we're beginning to see real financial trouble as the chain of goods and services begins to break down. Plants are closed in towns that had only one, families have no cash to spend, stores shut, banks close, and the new generation has to move on. When Phillips Petroleum, for example, with headquarters in Bartlesville, Oklahoma, had to fight off takeover raids by T. Boone Pickens, Jr. and Carl Icahn, it succeeded, but was left with $4.5 billion in new debt. Reorganization was imperative: 4,000 employees were let go and unemployment in Bartlesville rose from 3.9 percent in 1984 to 6.7 percent in 1986. On the plus side, Phillips did its best for its employees, and many took early retirement and remained in their homes in Bartlesville. And with so many highly skilled retirees, it might be that Bartlesville will sponsor the birth of several well-staffed service firms.

Nor are academic institutions and the nonprofits immune to cutbacks and organizational changes. During the last few years, both the Ford and Rockefeller foundations have reorganized—in some cases eliminating divisions; in others, replacing staff—but neither institution is fully recognizable as the Ford or Rockefeller of a decade past.

The New Corporate Pyramid

Many of us have heard a lot of talk about the corporate pyramid. Traditionally, the employee started at the broad-based bottom and scaled it as best he or she could, moving through the ranks of management trainees into middle management (or the academic or institutional or military equivalent) as the ranks thinned somewhat about halfway up the pyramid, and then, if one gained access to the stratum open to a lucky few, through the middle ranks to the narrowing triangle of upper-echelon management. A few super-fast-trackers could try for the gold spire atop the pyramid.

But during this decade of the eighties, the shape of the pyramid itself has changed. Parts of it are still intact—the broad bottom third, with young managers who are learning their trade, and the top third, staffed by those executives who have made it through the ranks and are reaping the benefits of survival. Mergers and acquisitions will eliminate some of the top management, but at least the tip of the pyramid still exists.

If one were to portray the pyramid schematically as it exists today, the artist would have to draw the middle third—the part that houses middle management—with great chunks taken out of it on two sides. Companies decrease staff where they believe they can best afford to, and many have surmised that the middle has more than its share of bureaucrats; no company will be able to afford a paper-shuffler any longer. Managers are going to have to produce.

Fortune magazine, in a special report published in the issue of February 2, 1987, referred to the new manager as being "value-added." The managers who remain will no longer be certain of promotion—there may be no place for them to go as the pyramid flattens—but they can count on being given greater responsibility. They will have to contribute to the profitability of the corporation in some real way as each division strives to become a profit center.

When the media speak of corporate America, they are usually discussing the more prominent companies—the Fortune 500, the Fortune 1000 and their competitors, as well as those larger companies in the service sector. These are the corporations that can afford to recruit on college campuses, and these are the companies that up to now have absorbed a great many of the best of recent college graduates and M.B.A.s.

But the diminution of opportunity for advancement within the best known of American corporations has not gone unnoticed by college and graduate students. Eli Ginzberg, professor emeritus of economics at Columbia, was quoted in the *Wall Street Journal* of May 4, 1987, as saying, "No sensible student of mine would join a corporation and assume they were there for life."

Recent graduates still prize the jobs at the large corporations, and compete to get them, but their expectations are very different from those of a generation ago. They think that good training is to be had in the big corporations, training they can make use of when they go on to managerial positions in smaller companies or start businesses of their own.

In the same *WSJ* article, Professor Howard Stevenson of the Harvard Business School describes a 1986 survey in which 90 percent of all Harvard Business School students said that they wanted to own their own businesses someday. These students obviously do not imagine a lifetime spent at a major corporation, which is just as well, because each fall corporations are hiring fewer and fewer recent graduates: 10 percent fewer in 1986, for example.

Downsizing and mergers and acquisitions and restructuring have been in force for several years now in this country, and hordes of managers have lost their corporate berths as a result. Enough time has passed for us to get some idea as to what is happening to those people.

What does all this tell us? Have middle managers become lost, struggling along in marginal jobs on the outskirts of the economy, or have they found ways to continue in a productive and profitable manner? And if they have landed on their feet economically, how have they done so?

The news, as reported in the financial press, from research sponsored by business groups and nonprofit organizations, as well as the results that we see here at Swain & Swain (86 percent of our clients find an opportunity that is better than the one that they left) is promising.

Your Choices in the New Economy

Sometimes our clients, especially those who are over forty, need help in interpreting the world around them. Some of them are not sufficiently aware to recognize the extent to which the working world has changed. It's a long way from the security of a specific, well-defined position in a corporation to the knowledge that you as a job seeker are probably going to have to depend on yourself—your own income-producing skills and your own ingenuity—for the rest of your working life.

We do not mean to indicate that corporate America has suddenly become an untenable place in which to work. But we should all understand that the new realities of the marketplace will prevent the cozy paternalism of a generation ago. Companies can't afford to make a lifetime commitment to their workers—the concept of cradle to grave care is gone—and those workers must learn to define themselves according to their skills and ambitions and not according to the corporation for which they work.

Because the expectations of the corporation have changed, yours must change as well. That doesn't mean that your career will be any less satisfying—it will simply be different.

We are not, after all, in the midst of a depression, although some industries are in trouble. Self-pity is nonproductive. There are jobs out there, and our experience here at Swain & Swain indicates that everyone who wants a job will get one. But your entrepreneurial spirit, your creativity—even if you are planning on returning to an office and not opening a fast-food franchise—are all traits that should be pulled out of mothballs and aired. It can be very exciting and satisfying to rely on oneself—the pioneer spirit is reviving in America.

But where will you take that pioneering spirit if you have been fired?

You can take it into a business of your own, if this is what you've always dreamed of and you have the personality, character, and backing to pull it off (see Chapter X for details). Or you can resume corporate life, although it may not be with the same sort of highly visible, well-known company that you've been working for in the past. If you were a manager for one of our major corporations, the sort whose name you knew as a child, then you were probably used to certain perks associated with the job, as well as having clients or suppliers pay attention to you because you commanded part of the budget of "Mega Corp." You had an expense account, perhaps limos to the airport, a health club membership, a desk loaded with state-of-the-art pencil sharpeners and VDTs, a secretary who was really all your own, a staff, and the respect of your friends and coworkers.

But you got terminated. And so did a lot of your colleagues. And the company itself is cutting back on "unnecessary niceties," and a lot of the positions are not being refilled, and the people who are left have not only lost their secretaries, but also are doing the work previously done by three.

That's the reality of Mega Corp. Also, they may be acquired and their top management dismantled or relocated. Or what was previously your division might be eliminated entirely. Don't look back. Things are not so tranquil and secure for those who stay with the company.

This is not to say that you will not get another job that is the equivalent of the one you had at Mega Corp. with the personal computers and glass offices that you had before. But this time you will be more wary. You will make the best deal possible, you will try to save some money, and you will keep your résumé up-to-date and your job-searching skills honed. You will continue to network—in an appropriate, discreet way.

You owe your new employer good value. Corporate executives seem to be complaining now about younger employees especially.

"They spend all their time having lunch and getting ready for the next job," said one manager who headed a large division. "Sometimes I think this department is a training ground for teaching upward mobility—outside the organization!" That manager is not going to give any of his slick young employees a solid recommendation, so do remember to pay good attention to the job you have at the moment. They're paying your salary, and after all, that's the springboard from which you'll look for your next position. If you are let go for any of the many reasons we have outlined above, you will need their help.

Remember that Mega Corp. is not the only game in town. It may be time to think creatively and contemplate recent news from the Small Business Administration. A small business is defined by the SBA as having no more than five hundred workers. Small potatoes when one is used to the international scope and numbers of Mega Corp. Yet, there is strength in smallness, and small businesses in the United States are responsible for 38 percent of the gross national product, 42 percent of all sales, *and* 48 percent of private employment. That's almost half. And they're looking for good people with experience and judgement—now.

Scott Benjamin represented everyone's idea of a "whipped dog." Kept on the shelf for more than ten years in his stalled position at a large investment bank, his sense of self-worth and self-confidence had deteriorated seriously.

When he was finally terminated, Scott felt discarded and unworthy. What he failed to understand was that many smaller and less well-structured financial organizations would welcome and appreciate his larger-company experience—even if he felt a little uncertain about his own value. Not surprisingly, a recently founded brokerage house needed someone like him to help them organize their systems and customer services function.

As he sensed the challenge during the interview, Scott revived like a long-unwatered plant. He actually regained his former sense of self-worth and received an offer that included the opportunity to manage the office, which would showcase his administrative skills.

In an interview in April of 1987 on the "MacNeil/Lehrer News-Hour," Marshall Loeb, managing editor of *Fortune* magazine, talked about the results of what he called the "epidemic of corporate raiding." The results, added Loeb, will be the increased need of American corporations to become more competitive, which will involve the kind of downsizing that we've discussed above. Where should the ousted managers go? "Smaller is better than bigger," advised Loeb, "and service is better than heavy industry."

Smaller may be better for a number of reasons. Most important, that's where the jobs are. Of the 250 managers surveyed by *Fortune* in their March 2, 1987, issue, 60 percent found jobs in a smaller company, only 32 percent in a larger company. Not surprisingly, 54 percent supervised fewer workers, even if their authority is actually greater. In our experience, 83 percent of the outplaced executives we work with secure new jobs in smaller companies.

Also, the nature of most jobs changed, sometimes leading to surprisingly intense job satisfaction. Of those surveyed, 61 percent went into a different business. *Fortune* interviewed Robert Freiburger, a forty-one-year-old ex-employee of ITT. As general manager of a division of Eagle-Picher Industries that makes liquid crystal displays, Freiburger is pleased with the change. His new management, he says, "gives us freedom from constant corporate review of everything. They don't believe in prolific memo writing, policy manuals. . . . They believe in loyalty of the individual to the company more than larger bureaucratic organizations tend to do."

The most important change discovered by managers who go to small business is that they often return to using those skills that got them into the workforce in the first place. Small companies, perhaps even more than the mega corps, must subscribe to the ideas of *Fortune*'s value-added manager. Rarely does one come across a middle or even top manager with only administrative duties. Employees often keep active, and functional, until retirement.

Marshall Loeb, in his interview on MacNeil/Lehrer, mentioned that service is better than heavy industry. Not only is it better, but that's where the jobs are, and will continue to be into the next century. The Bureau of Labor Statistics tells us that by 1995, 74.3 percent of all the jobs in the United States will be in the service sector—those jobs that include communications, finance, trade, government, real estate, transportation, as defined by The Bureau of Labor Statistics.

There are, of course, numerous corporations of varying sizes that are in business to supply these services, and some of you will find jobs with them, but it is a fact of economic life that staff jobs are becoming fewer, as companies realize that they can hire free-lance or part-time hands as needed, thus saving wasted down-time as well as the whole package of employee benefits.

The Two-Tier Work Force

The result is an economic phenomenon referred to by the *Wall Street Journal* as the two-tier work force—a work force comprised of those inside the corporations and the army of consultants that are outside. Eli Ginzberg of Columbia has called it a "core" and "peripheral employment" system. Those inside still enjoy benefits, and perks, although perhaps face an uncertain future; those outside have to look after themselves.

If you, on your own or in partnership with colleagues, decide that consulting in your areas of expertise is worth a try, if you want to see how you manage as the second tier in the two-tier work force, be warned there are some difficulties in looking after yourself. Think about the downside carefully, especially if you have come from the collegial atmosphere of a corporation, where have you been used to the feedback and companionship of your coworkers.

Below are some of the reasons for continuing to place yourself in a corporation—large or small—that will furnish you with the benefits that you would be uncomfortable without. Remember, too, that if you recognize that your overwhelming feeling would be one of anxiety if you forsook the protection of a company, you could view consulting as a stop-gap measure. Sometimes an association with a company as a free-lancer does lead to a job offer, or you could be engaged in a serious job hunt as you made some extra money consulting.

So, before you give up your interviewing, think about our list of deterrents.

1. *Income unpredictability.*   Some consultants actually do better than staff workers financially, but you will not be able to predict your income unless you have steady contracts with a number of clients. It's unfortunately also true that not all companies are meticulous about paying consultants within what you might consider a reasonable period. And pressing people for money is not one of the creatively satisfying events of a consultant's day.

2. *You may be lonely.*   Even if you have partners, there will be no office lunches, baseball games, company picnics, or new employees to socialize with. Networking, of course, will continue, but anyone new whom you meet will be through your own efforts.

3. *There will be no company-paid benefits.* If you have a working spouse, then you may still retain good health, life, and disability insurance, which you will discover can be prohibitive if you buy it on your own—it may even be impossible to get the excellent coverage that you've been used to. But if you have a consulting company with as few as three members, you can get group insurance. So, if you're forming a company, keep that in mind.

4. *You have to run your own office.* This means paying for everything, from paper clips to a copying machine. It means arranging for a messenger service, designing and buying letterhead, sharpening your own pencils, and pouring your own coffee.

   A new publisher, who had come from one of the great publishing conglomerates and went out on his own, told us once that he couldn't understand why all his start-up costs were so high. He was handling all the production costs for the books—printing, paper, typesetting, and so forth—and his publicity manager was in charge of buying all office supplies. The book costs seemed okay but the day-to-day outlay was staggering. Closer investigation revealed that toilet paper was being purchased from Bloomingdale's, a charge account had been established at the local French restaurant for the use of the staff—all six of them thought nothing of having the restaurant deliver lunch on a rainy day. Our publisher friend decided that his staff did not need *poulet en casserole* at their desks, they could go out and make do with Burger King. It had never occurred to him that his publicity manager would continue the lush ways she had become accustomed to at her previous job.

5. *In addition to office expenses, you will have to cover all travel and other business-related costs.* If you fly to Des Moines, it goes on your American Express card, not the company's. You pay for the rental car, and your hotel. The plus side: it's largely deductible, just make sure that every expenditure is documented.

If the above list contains problems that appear too formidable, if the implied lack of security is overwhelming, remember that very few corporations in today's economic climate offer any kind of reliable safety net. You could get another salaried position and then go through the corporate turmoil of reorganization that you've already survived once. On the other hand, if you try to build your niche as a free-lancer now, particularly if you're in a field that has demand for your services, you may achieve undreamed-of security. If you're still hesitant, do think about joining forces with others in a similar position—you'll have someone to share the risks; you'll have backup, invaluable if you're trying to expand—you don't want to turn down work; and you'll have someone else's imaginative energy to help you out.

The Creative Personality

The creative personality will be successful in the new job environment. By "creative" we don't necessarily mean "artistic," but rather inventive, spontaneous, flexible; a person who has learned, by observing the surrounding scene, that the old rock-rigid mindsets are going to lead exactly nowhere. It's the sort of creativity that has led some midwestern farmers who were caught in the farm crunch to diversify—forget cabbage and corn, these folks are raising mini-veggies for the very lucrative gourmet market.

When we counsel our clients, we stress the values of adaptability—willingness to try new ideas or to learn new skills. Many of our clients have talents that have been untapped in their work experience. Sometimes these hidden talents can be the foundation of a new career.

Everyone likes case histories—particularly those with happy endings, because they show that real people can make real changes and get real jobs.

Margaret Davies* is now in her late forties. She is a southerner from Atlanta whose ambition and interest in finance made her a yuppie long before there was such a thing. In the era when most women were getting married or going into publishing or applying to graduate school, Margaret went to work for a large bank in their trust department. Although she started out doing secretarial work, as time went on her supervisors recognized her analytic and organizational abilities and began to give her responsibilities for trust management. Her clients were women (naturally, as men could not be expected to be guided by a young woman in financial matters), most were older, aristocratic women, who responded to her brand of intelligence and genteel charm.

As time went on, and Margaret continued to get more responsibility but no promotion, she suddenly found herself in an unusual position. The women's movement had come of age. The bank had no

---

* All names in our case histories have been changed to protect our clients' privacy.

women vice-presidents, a situation that would have to be changed. But they had Margaret—a loyal employee, knowledgeable, with a devoted following of rich old ladies. Within days, Margaret was the bank's first woman vice-president.

In the early eighties, the large bank for which Margaret worked was bought by an even larger bank. They found they had too many vice-presidents in their trust division and Margaret, women's movement notwithstanding, was out of a job.

Twenty-five years down the drain? Not at all. By now Margaret knew quite a lot about finance. She also knew that she lacked certain skills needed for the current job market, a deficiency that was quickly made up by spending a semester at New York University to fill in the gaps—all of which was paid for by a generous severance package.

Margaret also had an extensive network of friends and colleagues to turn to for help. In only a short time she was snapped up by an investment counselor, to whom she brought several of her former elderly clients.

Margaret has, what we at Swain & Swain consider one of the most important traits when job hunting—adaptability, along with the conviction that what she knew how to do was salable.

Although Margaret did experience emotional pain when she was terminated—twenty-five years with one company made it seem like leaving home—she did find a new position for herself reasonably easily, and in her own field.

And consider Major Mark Amster of the United States Air Force. Mark was a career Air Force officer, entering the service upon graduation from college with an engineering degree. Mark thought that his career was absolutely predictable—twenty years in the service, gaining as much rank as possible, then retirement with an attractive pension at forty-two. Still plenty of time to start another career.

But the military, like absolutely every other institution in our society, is subject to the vagaries of the economy, and in this case our national budget.

Mark had reached the rank of major and had just completed a particularly satisfying three-year posting in Spain with his family. The Amsters returned to the United States to discover that the military establishment was in one of its cost-cutting modes, and all unnecessary personnel were being either forced into retirement or shunted over into the reserves, which in the military is the equivalent of being removed from the fast track. Without hope of further promotion, his career stalled. Mark resigned, with not an idea as to what he would do next.

Mark had had academic training as a mechanical engineer and had obtained much administrative experience in the military. He approached an executive search firm that specialized in ex-military officers to see if they could help him.

It was not long—about seven months—before Mark found something that he thought he would enjoy and that paid a good salary. He became the engineer in charge of running an enormous office complex in New Jersey. He was in charge of everything that made the complex go: electrical and plumbing systems, repairs, office services, tenant problems. Mark's wife was horrified at first—she thought of him as being a glorified building superintendent, and she missed the support systems inherent in military life—but in time she learned to enjoy the freedom of being relieved of the duties that burden an officer's wife, and also learned to appreciate the difficulty of Mark's job.

Mark was, not surprisingly, a disciplined, efficient administrator. Because he kept the complex's tenants satisfied, the ownership saw that he received frequent salary increases and substantial bonuses. Financially, Mark earned double his major's pay.

Although Mark misses the military environment, he has made the best use of his skills and has recovered from his disappointment. He overcame the mindset in which he saw himself only as a military officer, and found that civilian life has its rewards, too.

We cannot predict what sort of luck you will have in your job search. But others before you have had success, and may have even improved their situation. So, keep in touch with the creative, inventive aspects of your personality. No one will force you to take a job that you consider bizarre, but an open mind could lead to new and satisfying opportunities. The old corporate ways are dying, and you might as well accept the new with grace and enthusiasm.

Chapter II

How Safe Is My Job?
Your Survival Barometer

Chairman to subordinate: "How long have you been here, not counting tomorrow?"—[anon.]

THERE *is* upheaval in the ranks of America's businesses, and it may be that we are approaching a time of change as profound as the Industrial Revolution in the way that we look at ourselves in relation to our work. And as we discussed in Chapter I, the safe havens of lifetime job security are disappearing.

Large corporations are caught in a bind. Each day they must battle against foreign competition, competition from other megacorporations, rising costs, shrinking markets—there is no room for administrative fat, and cost-cutting and downsizing have become live-or-die necessities.

Economic considerations of revenue levels and program funding also have been affecting numerous nonbusiness categories—universities, nonprofits, health care organizations, government institutions, theatrical and other creatively based endeavors. There is no institution of any sort, even the most generously endowed foundation, that is not scrutinizing everything from its catering bill to its managerial costs.

It is to any organization's advantage to have a stable, loyal work force. It is also to its advantage for its employees to concentrate on their jobs, and how best to ensure efficiency and profitability, rather than to bumble through the workday in a panic, wondering if the job that was theirs on Wednesday will still be theirs on Friday. And sometimes the worst *will* happen unexpectedly. Indeed, about 20 percent of our clients felt that they had been blindsided by their employers. One moment the happy employee, the next the recipient of bad news, followed by a "Who, me?" gasp of horror and astonishment.

Companies do not plan to disrupt the lives of their employees, but these are uncertain economic times. What we try to impart at Swain & Swain is a practical approach to the realities of the working world. As we mentioned earlier, any member of the business community is probably going to be fired at least once. There is no way for you to accurately predict whether your company will have a bad quarter, or be bought by a Dutch multinational, or decide to eliminate a department. A company's business is to stay in business—and sometimes you will get caught in a reorganization that affects you negatively. You *can* learn to sense the winds of change, and to assess your vulnerability with hard-nosed accuracy. Change is much easier to bear if you're prepared for it.

Take Stock: Your Company in the Economic Matrix

As you try to assess your personal position in the economic scheme of things, it's perhaps wisest to step back from your own situation and look first at your company's strength within its own industry, as well as the health of your industry nationwide, perhaps even internationally. After all, if your corporation is swallowed up by a multinational, your relationship with your current boss may not matter at all. You'll probably both be looking for work.

Review and codify what you know about the state of your corporation and your industry. This sort of exercise is never a waste of time. Reassessment can clarify your thinking. You may, for example, realize that although your company seems to be growing, your training is left over from the last work generation, and if you want to have a business future at all, you may have to retool your skills.

What are the questions that you should answer as you assess your industry's place in America's economy and try to predict its future?

IS IT A GOOD TIME FOR BUSINESS IN GENERAL? As of this writing in 1987, the United States has been enjoying both low inflation and low interest rates. But with increased competition from abroad, many industries are feeling the pinch in their global environments: their response is to modify spending of all sorts, which often includes massive cutbacks of personnel. And, there is the uncertain impact of Black Monday outside the stock exchanges.

What about your industry in particular?   Even if you are in a growth industry it is no guarantee that your company will not eliminate your particular job during a streamlining effort. It is hard, particularly for older managers, to realize that they might be terminated even if their department is productive, and they are loyal, efficient, amiable employees. However, you are obviously in greater jeopardy if your industry in general is not doing well: all the petroleum-related industries, airlines, automobiles, steel, and many other heavy industries are facing declining profits or enormous losses, and are showing a great many executives the door.

Are you in an unstable industry?   Do you, for instance, work for one of the last remaining independent publishers? The chances of there being at least a takeover *attempt* are pretty good, and although the promises are always the same—"We're delighted to be joining forces with XYZ management. We're sure that we will all work productively together"—the honeymoon often ends abruptly. A new management has its own goals, own people, and will surely stick with those whom they know rather than fly to others.

Is your company floundering in an otherwise growing industry?   It may be due to poor management, premature expansion, ill-advised change of product, any of the evils that business is heir to, but it's more sensible to devote your energies to a growing and expanding business than to one that is dying.

We recommend frequent reassessments of this sort so that you can train yourself to see the handwriting on the wall. If, for example, you work for a company that has been making hand-powered lawn mowers since the 1930s, you should not wait for them to go into receivership—but get your job search started immediately.

Now restrict your field of vision. Has there been upheaval or business reverses in your own company on any level—involving top management or departmental organization?

Has your company been taken over?   It may be that you have been bought by a corporation whose base is in a different industry. This may work to your advantage, and bring your company needed cash and, concomitantly, the opportunity to expand. Or you might have been bought as a tax loss, or for the parent company to acquire a large debt to discourage unfriendly takeover attempts—in either case, you might expect benign neglect, but your job will probably be safe.

Has your company merged with another in the same field?   As we mentioned above, this could mean big trouble. A common corporate method of choosing the managerial survivors is the "club sandwich" approach. One layer comes from one company, the next layer from the other. If the two companies have different styles of management—which is most likely—difficulty may result. And of course you don't know if you will be part of the sandwich or in the soup.

A little closer to home, does your division or department have a new boss?   And does he or she want to bring in a new management team? Or perhaps your styles of management just don't jell? You could try to adapt, but if you're quite set in your methods of management and problem solving, you may become involved in an adversarial relationship.

If you find yourself in any of these potentially difficult situations, we are not suggesting that you fold up your tent immediately. But you might just start rethinking your future and what stance to take in perhaps repositioning yourself for a new job or career.

Are You at Risk?

It may be that you don't care profoundly if you are fired. There are those who are not happy with their current situation; there are those who are contemplating a career change, a return to academic training, early retirement, a stint with the Peace Corps. Some of these dreams are only that, some could become reality: we'll discuss practicalities in Chapter V, as our readers learn to get in touch with themselves as number one.

But what if you really need the job you have now, and what's more, you like it and think that you could have a future within your company?

You're going to have to face some hard facts. You may be pleased with your company, but is it a case of unrequited love? A phrase that we believe is fundamental in every area of life—and no more so than at the job—is "realistic assessment." It doesn't matter if you're a comparatively new employee or an old hand. The buck has stopped on your desk, and you should try to sort through the babble of corporate lip service to make an assessment of your position. As you pursue your daily routine, brush away any cobwebs that may be obscuring situational realities.

You will naturally discuss your situation with close colleagues, friends, spouse—you must remember that these people have your best interests at heart. But they also want you to feel okay about your job, and yourself, and rationalizations may creep in. You can talk yourself into any frame of mind if you overanalyze and misdiagnose and perhaps look for positive signs that don't really exist. Your significant other may not be the best person to decide whether or not your job is safe—only your employer knows for sure. But treasure the opinions of those who respect you; they are your emotional support system, and if you find yourself in an emotionally draining situation, that is the appropriate time to rely on their advice and affection.

A few guidelines as you begin your investigation. First, don't assume that it "can't happen to me." American corporations and institutions are too much in flux for a competent performance on the job to be sufficient criterion for security.

Second, relax. We have discovered unequivocally during our years of working with clients with varied backgrounds that if someone *really* wants a change, there *is* another career opportunity out there. Your job search may follow lines that you had not thought of before, but creativity is energizing, and the end result is often better than the job you left.

Third, be discreet. Office gossip and rumors can get out of hand. Unless you have a colleague whom you know you can trust with your most tender secrets, gather what information you can from everyone, but don't complain about your situation and, most important, don't voice your fears. Anything you say can easily follow channels to exactly the wrong pair of ears.

Reading the Signs

How do you read the handwriting that is bound to be on the wall (and remember, it's seldom a forgery)?

Trust your emotions. If you feel uneasy about your office environment, there probably *is* something wrong. For example, what's been going on in the managerial ranks? Have other executives been fired recently? Obviously, if this is the case, you probably should skip directly to the first section in Chapter VII, "Assess Your Marketability."

Some signposts that portend trouble:

· Are there a lot of closed-door meetings going on, to which you have not been invited? Is your boss in conference, it seems, with everyone except you?

· Is your boss suddenly unavailable for the semi-social encounters you used to have, like lunch in the executive dining room?

· Have there been fact-finding trips to the plant in Colorado, to which everyone on your level but you was invited?

· Memos. These are an important part of corporate life because once something is in writing, it ends up either on a computer disk or in someone's file, and usually has to be acted on in some way. To get rid of it, it has to be shredded or erased, and we all know what sort of difficulties that can cause. It may be that you find yourself deleted from usual routing slips—you're being closed out of the informational network.

· Is a colleague who used to pick up the phone and say, "Hey, Roger, what do you think of the new guy in the Santa Fe office?" now strictly business? Are all communications from his office now in writing with a copy to the boss?

· Do you have to review your expense account with your boss, and do you find yourself having to justify every expenditure?

· Have you discovered that you're at the top of the salary range for your position and that there's no promotion in sight? Or, on the other hand, are you woefully underpaid, you know it, they know you know it, and no one is making the slightest effort to redress the problem? One foundation executive, when the annual salary review was conducted, was told that his raise would be 2.5 percent. After making a few inquiries, he found that he and one other executive were alone on that particular level—the average increase was 7 percent. They were both gone within two months.

· Or has your salary review been postponed? In the past, you've had productive sessions with your boss in which you'd negotiate a salary increase and he or she would critique your performance. The criticism was helpful, and because you felt that there was good will on both sides, you understood that any suggestion was in aid of improving a proficient and appreciated performance. But somehow this year the annual review has not yet happened.

· Perhaps you've been given what is clearly a suicide assignment. It was a bad product idea to start with, market research predicts a bomb, and the whole thing should have been canceled—but it wasn't and now it's your headache. Management may think that you're just the person to infuse life into the body, but they may also be grooming *you* as a scapegoat.

· Other members of your cohort are being promoted around you, while you're left with a three-year-old title.

· The background and skills of a new hire look suspiciously like your own, and he or she is younger and probably comes cheaper.

· Your area of responsibility has been diminished. Perhaps you now share a secretary, or have lost an assistant, or have been requested to move to an inside office.

Obviously, any of the above are serious trouble signs.

What Went Wrong?

There may be nothing you can do to turn the tide, but for your own peace of mind, as well as your future, it is helpful if you can figure out exactly what went wrong.

It may be that you are simply out of sync with your company. You don't understand them, and they don't understand you. We had a client not long ago who was a very laid-back southerner, a commodities wiz who had been on his own and then accepted a position with a conservative, old-line brokerage house. It was a case of a square peg in a round hole. Although his work was creative and thorough, it wasn't appreciated because his style was wrong for this particular company. He maintained flexible hours, his colleagues could hear him telling tall hunting tales on the phone to clients, and his general attitude was scarcely that of the live-or-die-for-the-firm sort of employee. After a year, he and firm agreed to part. He's now with a much smaller company, one that specializes in noncorporate investors. His outgoing, folksy approach is very effective in this setting and his career is going very well.

You may not, just as the laid-back southerner, fit in with the corporate culture in which you find yourself, but it could also be that you really cannot respond to the work itself. Although you may feel that your management skills can be applied to most business situations, you may not be able to drum up any enthusiasm for pet food, or cigarettes, or foundation garments. The solution is obvious. Take those management skills to a company whose product does excite you.

The problem could also be that you have not understood exactly what was expected of you. For example, some companies like to switch managers from line to staff jobs; some institutions insist that you have overseas experience before they will even consider you for promotion; some will not appreciate it if you refuse to relocate, or turn down a stint at corporate headquarters, which may be in an industrial park in a state that you wouldn't even want to visit. Look around you and see what the other guys are doing. By refusing to do what's expected of a fast-track manager, you may be relegated to a nowhere position with little chance for advancement. If you want to make a career with this company, and you think that your position is reasonably secure, you may have to compromise. You should count your blessings before you leave a reasonably appealing company.

Company needs do change, and you may find that your particular skills, which were in great demand when you took your current job, are becoming either obsolete or less vital to the direction that the company is taking. The American automobile industry is used frequently as an example of an industry whose needs have changed radically. After years of neglecting the development of cars that would prove tempting to the American public—a public that turned to imports in their frustration—the industry is cutting back drastically on its top-heavy marketing personnel as it begins to spend more money in a basic area—new technology.

However, your situation may be more serious than finding yourself in a company in which the direction has changed—you may be in a truly dead-end situation, with no one interested in your goods or services. We know of one woman, Barbara Da Prato, who has made a most successful career switch. A Ph.D. from Yale, she had been a professor of Romance languages for fifteen years. Barbara, like most mid-career academics, found herself in an impossible situation—there were no tenured positions available in her department, mostly because there was little demand for the courses taught. With tenure not forthcoming, she was forced to take her skills into the corporate world. After a couple of mismatches—which helped her to learn how business America worked and what she could offer—Barbara finally got a position as a supervisor in the communications department of a large maritime supply company, that is satisfying to her and makes good use of her teaching and supervisory skills. Although she misses her students, it is no small matter that she now makes three times her salary as a professor.

Your problem may be nothing more than the fact of your being a woman in a male-dominated field. There are three possible solutions:

- You can leave, and enter a field that treats women with greater equality, where you can expect regular promotions on an equal basis with the men, and in which you will find other women executives.

- Secondly, you can fit in—show the others managers that you can "be one of the boys." This works in some fields that are not too solidly masculine—but many women feel that the trade-off for even partial acceptance is too high. They see no reason why they must do all the adapting—it's the traditional "go along to get along" attitude that Congress tries to instill in new members. Some women do not feel that they should have to be more malleable than the men, or better sports, or more anxious to do the dirty jobs, or discriminated against in any way.

- Or you can be a trailblazer. You may *want* to be the one who forces a conservative company to have an executive washroom for women. This is an entirely different matter, and the subject for a different kind of book. You are, no doubt, already knowledgeable about your legal rights, and also have some idea of the obstacles that lie ahead. You will know how to set goals—parity of salaries between men and women, more women on managerial levels, opportunity for real advancement for women beyond the middle of the pyramid. As the presence of women in middle and top management increases, you will find more allies to help you. But do not expect thanks from your employer, and do not be surprised if you find yourself forced out anyway. The gender question is explored in more detail in Chapter VIII.

Which Will It Be?

It's been established by you and your colleagues that unwelcome change in your workplace is definitely a-brewing. These types of corporate change usually fit into one of three categories:

1. *Benign review:* "We have to improve the bottom line, so let's all tighten our belts and see what we can do";
2. *Realistic reorganization:* "We've become too fat around the middle, and we're going to have to reassess the productivity of managers at that level"; or
3. *Ruthless decapitation:* "The axman was seen checking into a small nearby hotel and the aristocrats fear for their lives."

It may be that you will be caught up in one of those everybody-goes bloodbaths (which we want you to be prepared for, because takeover and mass firing can descend like the hordes of Genghis Khan), but it is more likely that the company will talk of "reorganization" and maybe eventual cutbacks and you will have time to gather your thoughts.

1. Benign Review: Although management is rethinking their operation slowly, methodically, they may come to a decision that more extreme fixes are necessary. When the status quo changes at all, that is your signal to do some reassessing of your own.

Change often is the parent of more change, and we return to one of our basic premises: It is risky personal management to ignore signals of potential instability—the signs will be there if you know how to look for them. If you like to think figuratively, contemplate expert surfboarders. They are skilled in keeping their balance no matter what the changes in the surge of the wave they're riding. That's what we want for you.

As an employee, you probably view your job in one of three ways. You hate it, like it, or are ambivalent. If you are really unhappy, imminent change might make your situation better, and you would be smart to hang on. But if you predict an even more untenable situation, then turn to Chapter VII and get your new-job campaign started.

If you are not sure *how* you feel about your job, this might be an appropriate juncture to reexamine your career path—see Chapter V for some tips on organizing such a reassessment.

But what if you enjoy considerable job satisfaction and still feel that you have a long way to go before you have extracted all the experience you can from your current position? What guidelines should you follow to ensure that if there are cutbacks, you will be among the survivors?

LEARN TO BE A POLITICIAN—COMMUNICATE.   Think of a citizen running for city council or mayor. This person is *visible*. Whether your old management is reorganizing (and, remember, although a great many of our clients do come from corporate America, *all* of this country's institutions, from foundations to schools, are economically concerned and are thinning managerial ranks) or your company has been bought by another, you want top management to know who you are and what you do. This will require honing all your communication skills. You are going to have to speak in public and you're going to have to write.

Go to every meeting, even those boring ones that you used to avoid because they were "a waste of time." If reorganization is in the works, no gathering that includes your bosses is a waste of time.

You should be prepared with all the hard facts that you can muster and be accompanied by your best assistant to back you up in an intelligent manner and demonstrate that you can delegate and build an efficient team. Be strategic, don't venture an opinion on a subject that you don't understand in depth. Maintain your good humor under what may prove trying conditions, and don't argue with anyone. On the other hand, sycophancy is out. Do not grovel; it will not help your cause and you have to live with yourself.

In the past, you have been asked to speak to local organizations or to other divisions of your company. This is a time to say yes to every invitation, or even encourage them.

It may be useful to invest in a few coaching sessions with an expert in public speaking, especially if you suffer from anxiety at the thought of talking to an audience larger than your immediate family. Most executives do have to address groups of various sizes in the course of their workday, and the majority list public speaking as one of their most unpleasant tasks. It is good sense to learn how to speak more effectively—you may even begin to enjoy it, and the ability to take charge of a meeting in a poised way advertises you as an effective executive. Learn to do it right.

Every executive has to write memos, reports, and letters. If your fingers dance along the keys of your word processor, turning out balanced, clear sentences first time around, then you're among the fortunate few for whom written communication is not a problem, and perhaps even a pleasure. But if you still suffer from the same writer's block that you did in the fifth grade, and a status report is no easier for you than was a report on Coronado's search for the Seven Cities of Cibola, try to remember two rules followed by professional writers who have to work against a deadline day after day:

1. *Give yourself a finite time period in which to write your first draft*. This does not mean "sometime this week." It means Tuesday evening.
2. *Then*, write. First, of course, make an outline, even if it's very rough. Then get something down on paper or disk. You can always edit, or change, or redo. Those first few thousand words are the toughest, but it gets the muse clicking along.

Whatever you write should be as short as possible to still get your message across. If you have a word-oriented spouse, friend, or colleague, get some editing help. Remember that less is more in this case and most of those "helping" words that you learned about in that same fifth-grade class can come out. You need a subject, action verbs, and objects in a sentence. Adjectives are often superfluous. Do not meander. Establish your thesis in the first paragraph and then stick to your point. When you have, in your opinion, proved your case, and have been as informative as you think you need to be, stop. Stay away from hyperbole and simile—this is *business* writing—and take a stern look at your opening and closing paragraphs. These are the places where most writers engage in flights of fancy, and if you have, cut them.

During this benign review within your company, it doesn't matter if you're facing familiar management or new corporate owners, you want to position yourself and your department effectively; you want to be noticed favorably; and you want policymakers to understand what you do and why it's important.

If the management that hired you is still in charge, this is a good time for a status report—you may submit one periodically, anyway. In your report, you should summarize as concisely as possible what you've been doing and why it's important to the overall corporate picture. Be specific. Stress your department's proven ability to problem-solve and adapt. After all, if management has change in mind, you want to appear the essence of competent flexibility.

Are you dealing with new management? Introduce yourself and your department. It may be wise to wait a few weeks after the new team has taken over to try to ascertain in what direction they might be trying to move the company. If you can pick up even a clue, that is the direction in which to aim the thrust of your report. But, as with old management, what you must point out in your departmental description is your team's ability to solve new problems (this can apply to research, sales, production, line jobs, staff jobs—managers solve problems; that's what they're hired for) and to demonstrate flexibility in solving those problems and meeting objectives. If you've been with the company a very long time, it may be imperative to downplay that longevity and instead concentrate on what "you've done for them lately." New management is often not interested in keeping the old guard. After all, "if the old guard was so effective, then why is the new guard there?"

Do not despair if new management comes in and you cannot figure out what they want and what your place in the corporation might possibly be. No matter what happens, a recent study by Harvard Business School professor, John J. Gabarro, shows that you probably will have up to a year and a half to catch your breath. It's true that some reorganization will take place after only six months, but the greatest numbers of organizational changes, says Professor Gabarro, occur after eighteen months. By that time, you may have decided that you want something quite different.

ABOUT A VACATION AND OTHER TIME OUT OF THE OFFICE.   A long weekend is okay, but this is not the time to spend three weeks showing the family around Sicily. And this probably isn't the time to attend the "advanced management program" at Harvard. Postpone this, don't cancel it. Obviously, along with your concentration on increased visibility, you have to *be* there to make that campaign work.

LISTEN AND LEARN.   This is a time to gather information. If you interview any job applicants, pay close attention to what they say about other corporations. These companies may turn out to be just the place for you eventually. Listen to industry gossip, read the trades, the *Wall Street Journal*, all the traditional sources for business news. This is also the time to reestablish ties with friends and colleagues. This should be done, however, in a low-key way, as it's too early for your superiors to get the idea that you may be looking around. If they are thinking of cutting back, and you seem dissatisfied, you will be one of the first to go.

BE RECEPTIVE TO ANY INQUIRES ABOUT AVAILABLE TALENT FROM EXEC-
UTIVE SEARCH FIRMS. Attractive opportunities sometimes land on your plate long before you're even thinking about dinner—you are, after all, still employed, which by definition means that you are still in demand. You must remember that executive search firms are not employment agencies. They are paid by the corporations and usually most of the people they place are currently employed by other companies. Do not write them off, but if you find yourself out of work, don't expect too much of them. The executive search firms will certainly be interested in you if you happen to match the needs of a client, but they are not going to find you a job. They will naturally concentrate on the objectives of those who pay the bills—their corporate clients.

"We do look at résumés," says Paul Slater of the executive search firm of C. Paul Slater & Associates. "It would be short-sighted and certainly counterproductive not to. Most of the better search firms do a pretty careful job of screening unsolicited résumés and, from time to time, a person's qualifications and an active search that the firm is working on match up with great results. Remember, a good search firm is always seeking qualifications that the corporate client feels are essential for the specific opening in its corporate structure."

UPDATE YOUR SKILLS. Does your company offer training in fields related to your department's areas of interest? Courses in management, computer skills, accounting procedures, even foreign languages, might be available to you. If you think that any of the offerings—whether taught on-site or at some sort of nearby institution—might enrich your background and enhance your marketability, take them now, while the budget for such training remains intact, you're still involved in a more-or-less normal day-to-day routine, and you have the energy to concentrate on something new.

Assess *now* how well the breadth of your training and experience stacks up against that of others who do what you do. If, for example, you are involved in marketing and your training in distribution is skimpy, this would be a good time to invest in a course—fill in those obvious gaps that will be immediately apparent to an interviewer.

Particularly if you've been working for the same company for quite a while, and perhaps been stuck in one job longer than you should have been, you run the risk of being viewed by both your current employer or a potential new company as a fusty back number. It is absolutely crucial that you try to counteract this impression. If something new—a computer system, an experimental telecommunications system—is going on that is remotely connected to your area of expertise, get involved. It will give you new energy, and if the time comes when you do have to move on, you may find state-of-the-art knowledge of a new technology useful as you go through the interviewing process.

2. *Realistic Reorganization:* This is the stage that may follow benign review. The company has decided to downsize, or it has been bought by another, or some divisions have been sold off—whatever the cause, the effect is that some job descriptions are changing, some people are being fired, some are taking early retirement, some of your colleagues are not waiting to see what will happen but have found jobs elsewhere. With real change going on around you, the atmosphere is highly charged, and employees are anxious. This is a time to keep both your own counsel and a cool head.

DO NOT LEAVE YOUR JOB TOO SOON.   We are assuming that you still find your work fulfilling. Do not be precipitous. Elaine Goodale is a marketing specialist who works for the insurance subsidiary of a Fortune 500 corporation. She has survived *seven* changes of top management in three years. Among the least of her problems was never knowing where the new home office was going to be—San Francisco? Pittsburgh? Chicago? It was all very unsettling, but she's now a vice-president for marketing, several years before she would ordinarily have moved up from assistant VP.

It might also be pointed out—and Elaine is the first to admit it— that although she's reasonably accomplished in her field, she's not a Harvard M.B.A. superstar, but rather a woman in her forties who reentered the job market about ten years ago, after a divorce. Why has she done so well? "Circumstances," she says. "I was in the right job at the right time. The new management found me inoffensive, I was doing an okay job, I wasn't making *that* much money so that they thought I was overpaid. Basically, they couldn't think of any pressing reason to fire me, so I survived. I would like to see myself as a success story, but really it's been mostly circumstances."

We cannot stress enough the point that Elaine is making. There are always incompetent employees in every corporation or institution— those who have alcohol or drug problems, those who exemplify the Peter Principle and have been promoted past their level of expertise, those who are unethical, those who are lazy. And these people are sometimes fired for cause. But remember that they remain a minority—if you are caught up in a reorganization and find yourself out of work, *do not take it personally*. As Elaine says, these days, it's usually just a result of bad timing—you were in the wrong job at the wrong time. You will handle your job search much more cheerfully and efficiently if you do not feel that *you* did something wrong. You may have missed opportunities, but committed no major errors.

The business world can be impersonal and, yes, this is a dehumanizing fact of modern culture, but that doesn't mean you can't have satisfying personal relationships in an office setting. You must remember that when reorganization is contemplated, you become a functionary who represents a certain monetary investment by the company, which may decide that the return on their investment is just not high enough.

Now that we've warned you against being a sensitive hot-house plant, let us return to our earlier warning about leaving too soon. If the signs are murky and not easily read, don't negotiate a departure before you have to. You may be one of those who survive, and, like Elaine, may even benefit by skipping several rungs on the promotion ladder as those above you fall by the wayside.

MAINTAIN MANAGERIAL QUALITY.   During a time of reorganization, there are bound to be undercurrents of unease, even fear, unhappiness as colleagues leave, uncertainty. By contrast, be sympathetic and helpful to your staff. It is only smart not to voice your own feelings of insecurity. Discuss the office situation with your peers to some extent—you certainly want to gather as much information as you can. But distrust gossip, and don't complain, especially to subordinates. If you do, you may find that your authority is diminished.

Pay particular attention to deadlines, as this is no time to let your department's standards slide. To your superiors you display a facade that is efficient, business as usual. And if you have the kind of job in which you deal with clients, be especially solicitous, for two reasons.

As long as you're being paid by your employer, it is only ethical to give them best value, and it is also a good idea to look at the client's operation with new attention. Might they be interested in having you on board?

PROTECT YOURSELF AND YOUR STAFF.   There are certain guidelines that you should follow to make life easier for you and your team.

- *Put a lot in writing.* If you have never had a memo-oriented department, make sure that everyone knows to write them now. You want the chain of command to be clearly established and you want management to know that each of your staff pulls his or her own weight. You should also be sure that outlines setting forth complete job descriptions for your team are in the files—and be specific, give lots of detail and praise when it is appropriate; these may turn out to be the only accurate analysis available to management of what your group does.

- *Consult with your staff.* They should understand that you're on their side. Don't protect them from bad news—share your information. There will certainly be morale problems as colleagues are let go. Be sure that your people know they can depend on you for recommendations if needed.

- *Review your own files.* Even though there has yet been no indication that you may be asked to leave, remove *now* any important personal material you may have in the office files. We've all heard horror stories of imaginative terminations, and we all fear being given half an hour to clear out our desks—with a security guard standing by—or coming in on Monday morning to find telephone and office furniture gone, our name off the door, and the painters renovating for the next tenant.

  Go through your files with an eye to your own future elsewhere, even if that day never comes. Take home a copy of every report, project, ad campaign, whatever it is that you produce that is portable and that showcases your managerial and communications skills. Graphic designers always obtain a printed sample of their work for their portfolios; you should have the equivalent.

  Get printouts of any material stored in the computer that you might need. Needless to say, this does not mean taking your company's mailing list, or other confidential material, but there are no doubt myriad items that are not sensitive that you could use as samples of your work.

- *Copy your Rolodex.* You should have in a safe place out of the office every business name and number that you might want in the future.

· *Get into some heavy-duty networking.* When the idea of change was more of a passing thought, you polished up your network of colleagues and friends. Now is the time to pull out more stops and do a reasonable amount of lunching. You want to know what's available out there and the more people you see and get to know, the better. But be careful not to be premature. You have, after all, not left your company yet, and you may not. Don't ask for favors before you really need them—you may not be able to visit the same well twice. You are not yet looking for a job. These meetings are to renew contact with people whom you may want to talk with in the future. All you want to do at the moment is to establish a congenial relationship with them. You want them to know who you are.

· *Review your finances.* If you have a spouse, talk with him or her; see your stockbroker and accountant. Prepare yourself for the worst possible scenario—you're out of work and are not sure what you will do when your severance pay is exhausted.

Make a budget. What perks will have to go? Does your company pay for the leasing of your car? For a country club membership? What are your rock-bottom monthly expenses? You should know all this now, before you're in a crisis situation.

THINK CREATIVELY.   As part of our counseling at Swain & Swain, we administer a number of assessments that aid our clients in trying to decide what direction he or she would like to follow. It is not carved in stone that you *must* try to land a job identical to the one you have just lost. It may be that although you're a CPA, you've hated the numbers-juggling that you've been doing all these years and think you would like a more managerial job. Why not?

You might want to test the consulting waters now, just to see if you like it and if there's any immediate work available for you. If you can find some free-lance assignments, you will be much less anxious about finances.

3. Ruthless Decapitation: There's not much you can do at this stage. You have tried to prepare yourself by expecting the worst, but it's hard to keep cool as you see heads of friends and colleagues littering the ground.

If you know that not everyone will be let go, and you still feel that this might be a good place for you, we recommend polite confrontation. Ask your superiors what's going on. They might be straightforward with you, and you may come away from the meeting with a realistic idea of your position. If you get nothing but mush-mouth evasion, you're probably on the termination list, or they *may* not have made up their minds, but you should start thinking about the severance package you're going to need and also start planning your job-search campaign.

If your particular situation does indeed turn into a time of transition in your work life, remember that change often leads to unimagined growth and new opportunity—it's up to you to remain flexible and optimistic as you try to identify that new opportunity.

Chapter III

The Aftershock: Dealing with Getting <u>Fired</u>

I have a new concept. I'm only going to dread one day at a time.—[anon.]

THERE are certain powerful, if superficial, indicators by which the world knows us and by which it assigns us a place in society—the way we look, the way we behave—known currently as "lifestyle"—and what we do.

In some milieus, what we do—our profession—is what we are.

Human relationships work best when there are no surprises and, indeed, the strength of any society is based on predictability. In order to interrelate, people need to know what guidelines to follow—and are comforted by the knowledge that the other person is following them, too. When the signs are not clear, and reciprocal behavior not certain, we enter a state of stress. Think of tourists in California driving along a highway who are suddenly surrounded by a pack of Hell's Angels on motorcycles. It may very well be that the gang will wave and fly on by, but the outcome is not certain—and hence stressful—because the Hell's Angels may not abide by the tourists' standards of behavior.

And so it goes in most areas of conventional life—we like to be able to recognize our allies and also to be able to place them correctly in the social strata.

If we know where a person lives, for example, and where he buys his suits, then we often assume other things about him as well.

If society forces us to adopt a certain diagnostic perspective, no identifying trait is more telling than what people do. Joseph is not just Joseph, he's a doctor. Anne is an account executive, and only incidentally about half a million other things. Philip is an electrical engineer.

After a while not only does society see Joseph as primarily a "doctor" or Anne as an "account executive," but they see themselves that way as well. The "professional them" becomes their most important identifying mark—the one that each individual presents first to gain instant acceptance and recognition.

With this powerful system in place, a loss of a job could mean a loss of identity, a loss of position in anyone's particular surroundings.

Gertrude Stein once said something like, "I am I because my little dog knows me," which was all very well for her to say—but in addition to her little dog she had a lot of public recognition as well.

But how do you feel if you are one of the many executives in today's market who is suddenly cut loose by the corporation or institution with which you identified—perhaps for years? You may well feel that your little dog knows you, but no one else knows or cares.

The First Stage: Shock and Depression

What do you lose in addition to your job when you're terminated?

Dr. Elaine M. Duffy, clinical psychologist and vice-president of Brittain Associates, human resources consultants, has talked with us about the sorts of deprivation that occur.

Not only does the employee experience the "deprivation that consists of the loss of social supports inherent in the job setting," says Dr. Duffy, "but also loss of salary and the sense of achievement as related to job performance." The result, she points out, can have a traumatic effect on a person's self-image.

"Most of us have been on the job for a long time," continues Dr. William Brittain, director of Brittain Associates, "and a lot of things that we see as rewarding come from the job: our feelings of accomplishment when we have a positive impact on the bottom line, the verbal pats on the back for having done a good job."

When your performance is no longer recognized because you're no longer performing, you may feel a profound sense of deprivation. Dr. Duffy explains that when an employee suddenly lacks the reinforcement that he or she had always depended on, that person may experience what behavioral psychologists call "learned helplessness."

Psychologists, in looking at a person's entire life—including and beyond the province of work—consider the feeling of control to be central to mental health. Jerry Burger, a University of Santa Clara psychologist who formulated a well-known scale that measures people's desire for control over their lives, was quoted in *The New York Times* (October 7, 1986), as saying, "We have a deep need to feel competent, to be in control of our environment; it is one of the primary motives in behavior."

Although theoretically the loss of a job should not encroach upon every area of a person's life—work, after all, is only one thread of what makes up a person's existence—in effect, it usually does.

The terminated employee has, after all, lost control over three absolutely vital areas of his or her life—control over:

1. *Being successful.* There is no benefit in our society to being unsuccessful. That doesn't mean that all cultural and economic environments have the same standards: in some, prestige is not necessarily equated with money—an instructor at Harvard, for example, enjoys plenty of prestige, but is not nearly as well paid as he or she would be if engaged in private commercial enterprise.

   But each field has its own guidelines for success—how many sheep can you shear in an hour; how quickly you can increase the value of a customer's portfolio—and in none of them is lack of defined success treated with anything other than disdain.

2. *Being rewarded for performance.* When you've lost your job, you've also lost access to all that stroking that everyone grows to expect in the course of a workweek. You expected and received—unless things were going very badly—praise for a job well done. The praise was the carrot before the horse. It made you feel good, so you kept going at full tilt. Another good job, more praise. The result was a feeling of being appreciated and enhanced self-worth—a stronger and more confident you.

3. *Monetary rewards.* One of the problems in convincing people who have always worked to do volunteer work is that they are not paid with money. When one is used to receiving compensation for a job well done, it is sometimes difficult to take volunteer work seriously. The importance of any job is equated with how much money you might get for it.

   Voluntarism is not the point of this chapter, but we would like to note that the feeling of importance associated with the idea that your efforts are a contribution that someone is willing to pay for is central to your view of your own self-worth.

In addition to the lessening of self-esteem, a great many of you may have real financial worries. Unless you have some backup—a surplus of money in the bank or a working spouse or indulgent parents—you must face the frightening prospect of having to scramble to meet your financial obligations, and not quite knowing how to go about it.

Loss of control can be a perception and a real condition. The reaction to it may be a galaxy of attitudes and emotions that combine to slide you into that psychoneurotic state called depression.

Everyone who is fired experiences some loss of control—but the particulars of suffering that each endures can differ widely according to the emotional makeup of the individual.

What might you expect—or are perhaps experiencing—after you finally clean out your desk and leave your office for the last time?

You are probably angry—furious at your company or institution for treating you badly. You might also feel some relief—you're out of an unpleasant situation. But if the events that led up to your departure were prolonged and nerve-racking, you are no doubt emotionally exhausted. You may have watched colleagues depart before you and experienced their complaints and pain and uncertainty. You were already at a low ebb emotionally when your turn came, making you even more susceptible to the cluster of emotions that one might predict in such an unstable situation:

Feelings of helplessness.   This is a common component of depression and its paralyzing effects must be overcome before you can attempt an effective job-search campaign.

Feelings of rejection.   It's extremely painful not to be wanted—we all experience it in one way or another throughout our lives: we're nine years old and our best friend at school finds a new best friend; or we're twenty-eight and our spouse leaves us for another.

A sense of inadequacy.   It's important not to let this feeling influence other areas of your life. The chances of your having been fired for cause are remote. You were simply in the wrong place at the wrong time—you're still the competent person that you were before your employer decided to cut back.

Denial.   Some people who are terminated refuse to face the situation realistically. In their fantasies, they are sure that their ex-employer will recognize that a terrible mistake has been made and call them with an attractive offer—full of apologies. We call this a "hidden agenda." We don't always know if one of our clients at Swain & Swain has these thoughts, but when a job search doesn't take off, we investigate the possibility. The ex-employee has got to understand that "over" is "over."

Denial can also apply to your feelings. It would take a very special set of circumstances for you not to feel at least some anger and depression after termination—you must admit it so that the healing process can begin.

William Torrey lost his long-time management position with a major retailer. At the beginning of his outplacement he startled his counselor by saying, "Your materials are way off base for me. I'm not shook up or angry."

This comment, by the way, was only startling in that the verbal expression didn't match his outward demeanor (i.e., deepest gloom). Like it or not, losing a job after a long time—and with hints that your performance played a part—is traumatic for thinking, sensitive people. You can be expected to mourn and experience anger.

Unfortunately, in William's case, the signs of depression and denial were masking the anger he felt incapable of expressing. Consequently, William became immobilized by his depression, and dealt with the issue by taking the next three months off.

As time passed and the reality of no job settled in, the anger erupted and William brought a suit for age discrimination. Was this the case? Not in the opinion of his former company and, ultimately, a court. Now William added a tarnished reputation in his field to the loss of a job—and, remember, he started off "not being angry."

A sense of being victimized.   This is the nonproductive feeling that "After all I did for them, they dumped me." It's the "Why me?" attitude—that you've been singled out for special unfair treatment.

Guilt.   You may really feel that being fired was your fault. You may even be correct in thinking that you were not doing a good enough job—or your employer was not making an adequate return on his investment. Or you may blame yourself because you can't accept the idea of just plain bad luck—and you have to blame someone.

Feeling a fraud—you always knew that you were an imposter, and now you've been found out.

Research by a psychologist at the University of Pennsylvania Medical School, Dr. Joan Harvey, was described in a *New York Times* article (September 11, 1984). Dr. Harvey had recently told a meeting of the American Psychological Association that many outwardly successful executives are "victims of the imposter phenomenon [and] persist in believing they are less qualified than their peers. . . . Some very famous people have suffered from the feeling all their lives. . . ." said Dr. Harvey. "Richard Burton, for example, shortly before his death said that inside he felt he was just a poor boy from a Welsh mining town, and did not really deserve all his fame."

This phenomenon is equally prevalent with men and with women and might be exacerbated when an individual is fired—an event that merely reinforces their feelings of worthlessness.

Depression can be alleviated, but it has to be recognized first. Have you noticed yourself slipping into any of the patterns of behavior described below? If so, they are specific indications of depression and you ought to be aware of it. These feelings may pass in time as you organize your job-search campaign, but if not, seek expert counseling.

1. You wake up tired. You spend each day in a state of generalized fatigue and you have a much lower energy level than usual. You may attribute the fatigue to the too many drinks you had last night, but why are you drinking so much?

2. You experience decreased effectiveness and productivity in most areas of your life—in sports, for example, your squash game has fallen to pieces and at home your unanswered mail is gathering dust.

3. Because of your feelings of inadequacy, you may have adopted a non-characteristic self-deprecating way of talking.

4. Your powers of concentration have decreased—you can't finish a book and have a tendency to wander from room to room, unable to settle down to anything productive.

5. You've become socially withdrawn—you hate to answer the door or the telephone. Your spouse is becoming tired of taking messages from concerned friends.

6. You no longer find pleasure in the activities that used to be fun. Movies, dinner out, a game of tennis, an evening with friends—none of these interest you these days. You're restless and bored.

7. You're much less talkative than you usually are. You lose track of what you're saying and fall into contemplative silences.

8. You feel close to tears much of the time—you've even found yourself crying in frustrated irritation a couple of times.

9. You are negative and pessimistic—nothing is right; not your past, present, and certainly not your future.

10. You—or someone you know—may be talking about "how tiresome" life is. If suicide and death are mentioned and coupled with details about a possible method, even if they are mentioned in an abstract way, this may indicate the presence of definite plans. Also, the person who is truly intent on a suicide attempt may put his or her house in order—file important papers where they're readily accessible, review the will, throw things away. These are all important indicators and must not be ignored.

11. There may be physical side effects to your depression: you may have gained weight or lost weight; you may have started smoking again; you may be drinking too much or experimenting with drugs.

12. You may be neglecting your physical appearance; hair not trimmed, clothes not pressed— you've lost your old "look" that you're going to have to regain before you hit the job-campaign trail.

The Second Stage: Reentry and Recovery

If depression is a state of mind, then it can be overcome by changing that state of mind. Popular culture is full of quick fixes. During the 1920s, Americans were treated to the imported wisdom of French psychotherapist Dr. Emile Coué. His self-help formula, "Day by day, in every way, I am getting better and better," became the rage, to be repeated on awakening to establish the right frame of mind. In more recent times, we know Norman Vincent Peale's *The Power of Positive Thinking*.

The techniques postulated by these once-popular authors may seem a little simplistic, but we approve of their basically positive attitudes.

It is depressing to be fired—but it happens to a lot of people and they do recover their equilibrium and go on to new successes.

At Swain & Swain we do not expect instant recovery after the trauma of a job loss. Frankly, we distrust instant recovery. In fact, our program is set up so that our clients learn skills and self-evaluation during the first few weeks with us and do not plunge immediately into the social give-and-take of networking and setting up interviews. But we do expect a gradual realistic acceptance of each client's situation—once that hurdle is past, recovery to some degree is imminent and the job search can commence.

We know that a *complete* recovery from the shock of termination may take a long time. But neither our clients nor you can afford the luxury of wallowing in your grief and feelings of self-pity.

"Time does *not* heal all wounds," says psychologist Dr. William Brittain. "In fact, unless you take steps to replace your depression with more positive feelings, time will make it worse. You have to do something to change your focus of attention."

The easiest way to change your focus of attention is to think about something else. That something else should not be related in any way to your job loss. That was simply one of the many things that happened to you this year; one unpleasant thing among a host of positive experiences.

When you sustain the grief and guilt of job loss, you suffer a true emotional trauma. And like any other crises, such as death or divorce, you cannot predict with any surety the pattern or speed of your recovery.

You may recover reasonably quickly and feel somewhat better after a few months, or your reaction might be delayed. You could function efficiently for the first few months after termination and then suddenly experience emotional upheaval four months after the fact, just when you thought you were on your way to a new life. Be prepared for a setback, because no matter when your reaction sets in, you need time to grieve and accept your feelings of loss.

But once this period is past, nothing positive can be gained by dwelling on the details of your particular job loss—one of the suggestions that we make to our clients is to avoid commiseration with sympathetic friends, colleagues, and family members. You're going to continue to meet people whom you know well who have not heard the gory details. After a few months, and once you've started your job campaign, it's counterproductive for you to relive the trauma again and again. You will experience all that anger all over again every time you tell your tale. Lay the story to rest, and with it all those negative feelings that get you going emotionally every time you talk about the unfairness of it all. By this time you ought to have more positive things to think about and talk about.

Unless you have been *very* badly hurt psychically, and really do flounder about in pain until you decide to talk it out with a therapist, you probably can help *yourself* through the recovery period—with a little help from your family and friends. If, however, you are still unproductive after six months your depression may be pathological, in which case it is time to seek professional help.

The self-help techniques that we recommend are based on the autosuggestion that we talked about earlier: "Day by day, in every way, I am getting better and better." If you say you feel better, and that things are going well for you, you very often *do* feel better. There is a great deal to be said for putting on a good face.

Most of your healing will have to take place in your mind—you will literally have to talk yourself through the difficult first months of your job campaign. But there are some practical, commonsensical, day-to-day things that you can do, which, although no substitute for the return of inner confidence, may help you get yourself started living a more or less full life. At the very least, they will prevent you from thinking only about yourself and your own problems.

"Do something for someone else" is New York psychiatric social worker Dr. Jeanette Coin's prescription. "This might be your mother, or your kids, or a person who lives in your building needing help with grocery shopping." Although you will be spending a regular workday and perhaps more on your job-hunt campaign, you may have time to become interested in anything from local politics to getting rid of a toxic waste dump. You might not have had time to become involved in community service before and best of all, these concerns probably have absolutely nothing to do with your own problems. Working outside your own sphere of difficulty should help you put your own worries in perspective and, as a fringe benefit, you might even do some good.

Stay active.   Physical activity definitely has a place in your recovery process because it's another technique you can use to transport your attention to another plane. When you're trying to beat someone at squash, or playing one-on-one basketball, you're not thinking about that so and so who fired you.

Continue to go to your health club—the swimming and exercise will be invigorating, and the necessity for superficial social interaction is also beneficial.

Don't truncate your social life.   Give a dinner party. Take your family to Washington for the weekend. If your life seems normal on the surface, you will feel less adrift—more in control, which is the most necessary feeling that you must develop and nurture during your job hunt.

Reward yourself. Think of the people whom you know who never take a vacation or plan treats of any kind for themselves. You might even be one of them. They have a tendency to become self-absorbed and fixated on their jobs. Neurotic overconcern with the doings of their employer probably didn't save their jobs for them—or for you.

You're going through a bad time right now—let us continue to suggest that you plan pleasant experiences as treats; as rewards for sticking to your job-search schedule. Do something only for you: a day of sailing, a facial, a visit to an art gallery—whatever relaxes you and makes you feel pampered.

We recommend the above as simple day-to-day activities to give you a break, help you to have some fun—you really do have to lighten up during this period—and get the juices flowing with exercise; all of it will help you to think more clearly.

But the greatest help—without which you can do nothing in your campaign to reenter the work force in a positive way—must come from within.

In Chapter VII we will talk of your job campaign, but before you can undertake the specifics of that you must win a preliminary campaign to establish a sufficiently positive outlook on your situation and prospective job hunt.

Your technique to establish the kind of self-confidence that can be translated into action must be to focus on the positive, and relegate the negative to the end of your line of attention. You can start slowly, but start.

We asked psychotherapist Dr. Tessa Albert Warschaw how clients like ours could build the confidence that they need to conduct an effective job campaign. Dr. Warschaw pointed out that it's very important for them to realize that these days a lot of first-rate people are being fired. They certainly are not alone and should not wallow in self-pity or guilt. "I suggest that people take what I call an 'action step,'" said Dr. Warschaw. "This could be nothing more than reflecting on the really good job that they did for their company. Even reflection is doing something. It's a start."

This is a very important point. When you have been fired, you have a tendency to negate all the good work that you did while on the job. And in previous jobs. You should review your very real accomplishments: all the gains made for the company, all the money saved, all the projects successfully completed. It may even be that the company was very appreciative of all your fine work—right up until the moment that they fired you. We discussed earlier all the possible reasons for that—reorganization, downsizing, merger, cutbacks; it would be most unusual for you to have been terminated because of inadequate job performance.

Think: "Yes, I *did* help the company. . . . I did thus and so and I did it very well. . . . And I can do it for someone else."

The fundamental goal of recovery after termination is to regain control of your life. When you feel in control, confidence, enthusiasm, and self-sufficiency follow.

To begin with, control what is controllable. You cannot command a new job immediately—that is *not* within your power or control. But you can set goals for yourself—credible goals that mean something, but which are within your power to accomplish.

What sort of control is within your power? First, there is the control over your job search; and, second, once again you can control your rewards, which every adult ought to be able to do. How does all this work?

1. *You will organize your own database.* What you do during your job search should be documented—eventually you will build up your own library of reference materials. You will have a log of all your phone calls—the day and time they were made and what response you achieved; you will, of course, keep a copy of all letters. You will keep a diary in which you list and describe all meetings, and you will keep notes on your conversations.

2. *You will track the results of your efforts.* Control starts at the beginning of your job search: you are the one to decide how many phone calls to make, how many letters to write, how many ads to respond to, how many meetings to attend, how many appointments to set up. Your results will be in direct proportion to the quantity and quality of your effort—and it's all in your hands. Greater effort, greater response. You are certainly not helpless—there is always something else that you can do.

3. *You reap the rewards.* If you have made the sort of intelligent, honest effort that will make you feel good and will eventually get responses, then you will be rewarded. As people begin to get in touch with you, as opposed to the initial job search planning and development, the real

dynamics of a job search campaign begin. And with every positive response, your self-confidence will grow.

Positive thinking does work. If you approach an interview in a positive, energetic frame of mind—thinking all the while that the job is within your reach—and you look successful, then your results are that much more enhanced by your attitude. Corporations want positive, action-oriented people.

Dr. William Brittain uses a sports analogy to demonstrate the kind of confident approach that we try to encourage among our clients.

Professional athletes, says Dr. Brittain, must have a positive self-image—they visualize their successes before they happen; they intend to win. We've all seen world-class skiers before a downhill race, eyes closed as they run the race in their minds, imagining every inch of the course. They use autosuggestion to bring the victory to life for them—and it works.

As a job seeker, you need the same kind of mental preparation. If you respect yourself and your abilities, others will too; if you see yourself as a winner, you will be perceived as such—and you will win.

Your Support Systems

During this time of insecurity, as you work to regain your self-confidence and get back into the job market, you need to make the best possible use of the support system that's already in place for you: your friends and family.

Some friends or family members may have job leads for you, but that is not their primary function during this time—they are there to supply you with the emotional support that you need.

Women when they're in crisis tend to make better use of those close to them because they find it easier to ask for help and support, but men should make an effort to be open about their feelings—they need affection now, too.

Both men and women need to experience a sense of belonging—they've lost their identity in the work world and need to know that their place with friends and family is still secure.

The family is, of course, your most important support system. But one of your most difficult tasks during this time will be to keep your relationship with them strong and mutually satisfying. They will, of course, feel your anxiety. You may have financial problems.

It is very important to be honest with your spouse; your silence is more frightening than a realistic discussion of the difficulties and issues that face you: change in lifestyle, perhaps relocation, an uncertain future.

The average age of the men that we see in outplacement is in the early fifties; women are a bit younger. This means that not only are they contending with potentially serious financial and social problems, but they are doing it at midlife—the perfect time to have an emotional crisis of some sort as they try to sort out their future while negotiating the shifting sands of employment opportunities. It is not surprising that the divorce rate for people in this situation is quite high.

Think of your spouse and children as partners in your job search. Share with them. Ask for their understanding and help. Their respect and support are vital to your positive self-image. After all, your job was not the only element in your life. Don't let trouble in that area affect other aspects of your life. Your well-being is dependent on keeping as much of your life adhering to normal patterns as possible. Your family will help you in this as you participate in the normal give-and-take of your closest relationships. Don't withdraw and don't be careless of this most important part of your support system. A satisfying family life is your most important defense against the inroads of trouble in other sectors; if you have it, cherish it.

If you are a job-seeker with a spouse who is trying to help you both maintain your emotional equilibrium and also approach your job search in the most efficient way, share the rest of this section with him or her. It contains helpful tips that have evolved from the "spouse workshops" that Swain & Swain conducts from time to time to help husbands and wives of job seekers survive some difficult months.

How can a concerned spouse help the job seeker?

- First, think of your spouse, not of yourself. One of our clients had been president of a small company and had left when the company was bought. He was well-qualified and quite soon was presented with two job offers: one seemed right for him, as the number-two man in an industry that he was interested in; a well-run, successful company. The other offer was *president* of another small company, one that was in such disarray that he might not be able to put it in order during his contract.

But our client's wife was used to being "Mrs. President," and insisted that he take the second job. Unfortunately, it ended in disaster and our client was back in our offices to try again. A perfect example of self-centered, uninformed input that should be ignored.

- Try to protect your spouse from well-meaning but negative influences who want to commiserate with him or her.

- Try to keep a moderately active social schedule. You don't want to become recluses, but you don't want too much social stress either.

- Urge your spouse to talk about the job search; become knowledgeable about the techniques; ask to see the progress log. Become involved.

- Help your spouse communicate to your children that life will continue normally.

- Help your spouse research job opportunities, particularly if you know something about the field.

- Help with finances if you can; watch the budget.

- Share the truth with interested friends and colleagues, without dwelling on the negatives. Don't hide the fact that your spouse is looking for a new position; you never know where one might develop.

- Do not blame: Never, never say, "How could you do this to me?"

- Resist thoughts of vengeance; do not bad-mouth the previous employer.

- Concentrate on being realistic, resourceful, and patient. Understand that your spouse is under some strain, but this too shall pass.

- Show warmth and affection—you are your spouse's most important ally.

F.I.R.E.

With the development of the concept of F.I.R.E. at Swain & Swain, under the direction of Dr. William C. Stewart, we introduced a tool that our clients could use in order to measure their readiness to face the job market as realistic job seekers, able to analyze and make rational judgments.

F.I.R.E. is our acronym for those elements in human beings that make up character—the raw material that the individual uses in all relationships with the outside world.

The elements that make up F.I.R.E. are:

1. *Frustration tolerance*
2. *Impulse control*
3. *Reality perception*
4. *Ego boundaries*

If our client has good control over and understanding of these character traits—and has a clear idea of where his or her failings are and in what areas to be watchful—then we think they have a good chance of conducting a successful and realistic job search. If the job search *is* realistic, then the new position often works out. Of course, we want to avoid the revolving door of new job/outplacement/new job/outplacement, which could go on forever as people fail to become realistic in their expectations.

What should you look for as you think about these four categories?

1. Frustration tolerance.   Were you the kind of child who always got a new toy when the old one broke? Is the result that you're easily frustrated and extremely impatient with people and situations? One of our support jobs at Swain & Swain is to talk it out with a client who is feeling especially frustrated. A difficult time for this type of easily frustrated person is when a job search is not moving forward. If you fit into this category, try our method of setting small goals that you know you can succeed at. It will make the larger goal of employment more attainable.

2. Impulse control.   Do you go with what you feel at the moment? If this is a trait that you're familiar with, you've probably had a problem with it all your life. Think twice before you act. Anything that you can decide today could probably be just as easily decided tomorrow—make sure you have all the facts before you make a decision. It's very tempting to take the first real job offer that you receive, but do consider whether it's right for you. If you've gotten one offer, it's probably the result of all the seeds you've sown during the past months—others will come.

Haste really can end up wasting a lot of time when the job seeker is too precipitous.

Judith had been with her company for more than twenty years and had progressed to a successful career position in market research. A reorganization and relocation followed one upon the other and Judith resigned her position rather than move, having just married.

The time spent with the company and grade entitled Judith to twelve months of support, but a lack of impulse control reared its head. Because her experience was outstanding, Judith received an offer quickly. Unfortunately, the best offer seldom arrives first—and that was true in this instance. The new job would be significantly less demanding than the one she had just held.

Judith threw away ten months of additional support and took the first offer, saying, "I can't stand the anxiety of a job search." Her counselor argued, "But Judith, you'll be bored." Notwithstanding, Judith's campaign ended before it had a chance to flourish.

Three months later, Judith called us: she was bored, and thinking of quitting.

3. *Reality perception.* According to Dr. Stewart, this is one of the hardest areas to deal with. "Everyone's reality is different," points out Dr. Stewart, "and any individual may distort reality to fit his or her needs." If your reality perception is off, then you may end up taking the job that is wrong for you. As Dr. Stewart says, "The wrong job can be worse than no job at all, and you'll just end up back in outplacement."

This is one area in which you should seek out the advice of someone who has your best interests at heart. Use him or her as a sounding board and discuss what the likely realities of the job would be—that's one of our most important functions at Swain & Swain.

Flawed reality perception can also lead toward impossible goals.

David Schaller, a Swain & Swain client in his mid-fifties, had been a corporate attorney who had managed to make himself almost unemployable. A difficult personality, he had been generally disliked at his last job and had hung on much too long.

In his job search, he sabotaged any opportunity that came his way: he was rude during interviews, his letters were those of an illiterate.

David was in outplacement for almost a year before we figured out his hidden agenda. He really wanted to be rehired by his old company. He was tired of working and wanted to be bridged to retirement in a place that he knew. By his nonproductive behavior, he was telling his old employer that they would *have* to reinstate him because he couldn't find another job—a problem that had ceased to be of interest to the company.

David was an example of flawed reality perception—a narcissist who couldn't or wouldn't understand the real world.

4. Ego boundaries.   This is one area in which we try to ensure that our client can be objective—and will be so in an interview situation.

In a one-to-one relationship, each person has expectations. There may be some communication problems because what one person shows on the outside is not necessarily what he or she is feeling inside. It is important to establish some sort of common meeting ground between each ego so that realistic progress in negotiation can be made.

The techniques that we use at Swain & Swain are those that you can use yourself. The bases are self-analysis, self-control, and the ability to self-activate your job search.

In some areas, you will want the help of someone who knows you well—you may need feedback when you analyze the reality of a situation and figure out if it's right for you.

But most of the good things that will come to you during the process will be the result of your own efforts. By setting reachable goals, you will receive steady gratification; this ought to give you the impetus to maintain the energy level needed for a successful outcome to your search.

The Job Loss Stigma

During these new times, we at Swain & Swain have learned three, basic new truths.

The first—which gets proved again and again with each new client who arrives at Swain & Swain—is that there are no virgins left. *Everyone* who works for any period of time is going to lose a position sooner or later. This is a bet any gambler would be thrilled to cover—it's a sure thing. So if your turn has come, don't despair. You certainly aren't alone.

The second truth—*not* true ten or twenty years ago—is that the stigma that used to be attached to displacement is fading fast.

A few years ago, Swain & Swain tested the notion that the stigma attached to losing one's job was disappearing and sent a questionnaire to corporate executives and the search community asking what they thought. Overwhelmingly, they answered that being fired does not ruin an executive's chance for employment—however, the reason why he or she was fired is important.

In fact, 61 percent of the respondents felt that if a person lost a job, it was probably beyond the individual's power to control. In addition, they recommended that the applicants be rather more forthcoming about why the job was lost than they have been in the past.

The respondents felt that there were many acceptable reasons for moving on: among them mergers; emplacement of a new boss, one who may have come with a new team; the vagaries of the economy, necessitating cutbacks; drastic reorganization. These same respondents did not think that the applicant should disguise the fact of termination, but simply give an interpretation of the reasons as understood by the employee.

The third truth—and the most important—is that ways of thinking about one's own career, and viewing a relationship with an employer, and assessing where opportunity lies have all changed, probably forever. One way of looking at the current situation is to see the economic milieu as a world of disappointment and cutthroat competition. You have been fired and you're angry and bitter and scared.

But most people are not fired from the perfect position—you might have been working for the wrong company, or for the wrong boss, or perhaps even in the wrong field. We find that for many of our clients unemployment provides them with breathing space, a time to look at their life and their career and really assess the direction that their career path is taking.

Chapter IV
Your Job Search: How Long Will It Take?

Time (n.)—nature's way of preventing everything happening at once.—[anon.]

"WILL I ever find another job? With whom? Where? And *when?*

Most of our new clients are very eager for us to furnish them with the answers to these questions. Although we think that our job as outplacement consultants is to help our clients determine the answers for themselves, our years of experience in the counseling field have enabled us to make some predictions.

None of these questions is more important to our clients than *when?* When can I expect to be back on someone's payroll? How long will it take to go through this process?

Outplacement counselors have developed rule-of-thumb responses to comfort their clients and to give them some sort of framework for their job search. Perimeters of time are very important as the client plans his or her campaign. Even if the exact day, week, or month that one will reach the goal is not certain, the client has to believe that the goal is reachable or the campaign will never get started.

Some would-be pundits have suggested that the job seeker might expect to spend one month for every $10,000 of desired income: Do you want $60,000 a year? They would say, "Be prepared to invest up to six months." Others have simply given their clients the average length of a typical job search: somewhere between four and six months. But averages are not very comforting when you're a forty-nine-year-old man who earned $110,000 last year, you've been out of work for four months already, your severance package has only two months to go, you have children in high school and college, and the only steady income that you can count on is the $30,000 that your wife makes as a technical writer. That just isn't reassuring.

The OPT Predictor

At Swain & Swain, we found that these estimates were widely inaccurate, and of no use to anyone. But as the years went by, and our client list grew, definite patterns began to emerge from the increasing data that we gathered about every quantifiable element of our clients' job searches. Through brainstorming, trial and error, and an ever-expanding data base, we developed a predictor that we call the OPT (Out-Placement Time) that we have found to be extraordinarily accurate. OPT is drawn from the time it actually took hundreds of men and women to find new jobs in the years between 1976 and 1986.

Although simplistic formulas based on illusory samples apply to almost no one, we have found that if we factor in enough hard data specific to one client, we can predict with only a plus or minus 10 percent margin of error how long it will take for that client to find a job. With the elimination of guesswork and mystery, much of the normal apprehension associated with a job search is curtailed.

As indicated, the OPT forecast is based on data gathered from our experience with hundreds of job seekers over the past ten years: job seekers with all types and levels of education, men *and* women, various age groups, numerous racial and ethnic backgrounds, a variety of personalities, and diverse work histories.

Some of the factors, about 63 percent, associated with our clients are "givens"—age, time of year the job search starts, health, academic background—and some, about 37 percent, are variables—appearance, mental outlook, expectation—and are open to change if the job seeker is so minded.

Our calculations start with the observation that a job seeker needs a *minimum* of six weeks to get organized, send out letters and résumés, set up interviews, and if things go perfectly, receive an acceptable job offer. With six weeks as our base, we use OPT to determine how many additional weeks will be needed by either adding weeks for any factor that we have found to be negative or subtracting weeks for a factor that our experience has shown to be an aid in a job search.

For example, if a client is job hunting in the fall, the best time to look, we deduct three weeks from the search. We subtract another four if our job seeker has a superior network of contacts and another two because of an excellent educational background for his or her field. On the other hand, our example might be overweight (add three weeks), badly dressed (add another three weeks), and quite anxious about being too old or too young (plus four weeks). And thus we continue through our checklist of more than fifty items in six categories until our calculations are complete and we can predict with reasonable confidence the length of time our client can expect to spend in the job search.

Clients who come to Swain & Swain for outplacement do have the benefit of our counselors, who administer the OPT assessment and then interpret the results. Although you, the reader, are not trained in the analysis of the responses, we can give you an idea of the kinds of factors that we include in our six categories. We want you merely to note those factors that are a fixed part of your past and about which you can do nothing. Should they surface in an interview, present them in the best possible light if they cannot be considered an advantage—no college degree, for example—and concentrate on those variables, 37 percent of the total, that you can change for the better.

Your OPT Forecast . . .

You can achieve an answer to "How long should it take me to find another position or opportunity?" by completing the following pages. Be candid with yourself—and when in doubt, ask someone who knows you to help. (Check the case study in Appendix B, too.)

Read each factor description and circle the box that most closely represents your honest assessment of each factor at this point in your life. For example:

* How decisive are you about choices and direction?	VERY	MODERATELY	NOT VERY
	−3	(+2)	+4

As you see, the factor scored is "moderately." Many who have considered this factor are quick to point out that while they are normally "decisive" in their jobs, they become quite the opposite when facing career choices and direction for themselves. Thus, the appropriate answer given the extremes is: moderately.

Your Situation . . . Conditions and Circumstances of the Moment

Factors		SOMEWHAT	VERY MUCH
* If you have been ter- minated, how traumatic has it been for you?		+2	+4
		POSSIBLY	YES
* Do you harbor a "hidden agenda" (i.e., revenge, "I'll show them")?		+3	+6
	YES	MAYBE	NO
* Do you have access to "networks" and are you willing to use them?	−4	+1	+5
		MAYBE	YES
* Do you intend to make a career change?		+3	+4
	REASONABLE	NOT ENOUGH	CONSIDERABLE
Realistically, how much time do you have to find another position?	−2	+3	+6
		MAYBE	YES
Will there be a relocation involved?		+3	+4
	CLOSE	SO-SO	NOT CLOSE
How close are you to your targeted job marketplace?	−3	+1	+5
		SOME	SIGNIFICANT
Do any circumstances limit your job-search flexibility?		+2	+6
	UNDER 5 YEARS	5 TO 9 YEARS	OVER 10 YEARS
If you are an expatriate, how long have you been away?	+1	+3	+5
	FALL-WINTER	SPRING	SUMMER
What time of the year is it?	−2	−1	+3
			YES
Are you in a minority group (i.e., black, Hispanic, female)?			+4

*Indicates variable factor

Your Situation . . .

Factors

Will you be perceived as a
"fast-tracker" (i.e., salary
and title progression)?

	YES	POSSIBLY	NO
	−3	−1	+4

Your estimates . . .

Strike a total for each column, being careful to subtract −'s from the
+'s in each column. For example, if you checked the first box on the
left for each of the factors, you would have the following results: −4,
−2, −3, +1, −2, and −3 for a total of −13. Place −13 in the left box
of "Your total estimates . . ."

Your Style and Attitude

Factors

* How decisive are you
  about choices and
  direction?

* How do you think your
  confidence will be
  throughout a job search?

* How well do you
  tolerate frustration?

* How much are you
  affected by stress?

* What is your general
  outlook on life and
  work?

* Are you concerned
  about your age?

VERY	MODERATELY	NOT VERY
−3	+2	+4
HIGH	MIXED	LOW
−4	+2	+4
	SO-SO	NOT WELL
	+1	+4
	SOMEWHAT	VERY MUCH
	+1	+4
OPTIMISTIC	MIXED	PESSIMISTIC
−3	+1	+3
	SOMEWHAT	VERY MUCH
	+2	+5

	DEMOCRATI-CALLY	TO FIT THE MOMENT	AUTOCRATICALLY
How do you manage your jobs and others?	−4	+2	+5
		SOMETIMES	RARELY
Do your work habits exceed nine-to-five limits?		+1	+3
	GREGARIOUS	PLEASANT	SHY
How would you describe your outward manner?	−4	−3	+6
	MOSTLY	SOMETIMES	RARELY
Do you see yourself as a team player and do others agree?	−3	+1	+4
	AN OPPORTUNITY	MIXED	HAS TO BE PERFECT
How do you view a job search at this point?	−3	+2	+5

Your estimates . . .		

*Indicates variable factor

Your Abilities . . . As They Relate to a Job Search

Factors

* How well do you focus and prioritize?

VERY WELL	MIXED	WITH DIFFICULTY
−2	+2	+5

* How well do you follow through?

VERY WELL	MIXED	WITH DIFFICULTY
−3	+2	+5

* How are you in one-on-one situations and communications?

VERY COMFORT-ABLE	MIXED	UNCOMFORTABLE
−3	+1	+3

* How are you in stand-up presentations?

VERY COMFORT-ABLE	MIXED	UNCOMFORTABLE
−4	+2	+4

* How is writing for you?

EASY	MIXED	DIFFICULT
−2	+1	+3

* Are you a good listener?

ALWAYS	SOMETIMES	SELDOM
−4	+2	+5

* How often do you read "signals"?

ALWAYS	SOMETIMES	SELDOM
−2	+1	+5

* How comfortable are you with negotiations?

ALWAYS	SOMETIMES	SELDOM
−3	+2	+4

Your estimates . . .

*Indicates variable factor

Your Career History

Factors	4 TO 8 YEARS	UNDER 1 YEAR	OVER 20 YEARS
How long have you been with your present employer?	−2	+2	+4
	3 TO 5 YEARS		OVER 8 YEARS
How long have you been in your present position?	−2		+3
	2 OR 3	OVER 5	ONLY 1
How many companies have you worked for?	−2	+3	+4
	GROWING	MATURED	SHRINKING
What is the condition of your present industry?	−3	+1	+4
	GOOD	FAIR	POOR
What is the recent performance of your employer?	−2	+1	+3
	ADVANCING	FLAT	DECLINING
How will the outside world view your career path?	−3	+2	+3
	HIGH	MODERATE	LOW
What sort of demand exists for your experience?	−4	+1	+4
		MODERATELY	PROBABLY NOT
Are you considered current in your field?		−1	+3
	LINE	BOTH	STAFF
Will you be seen as a "line" or "staff" person?	−3	+1	+3
Your estimates . . .			

Your Health and Appearance

Factors

	EXCELLENT	FAIR	NOT SO GOOD
* What is your present physical well-being?	−3	+1	+5
		SOMETIMES	FREQUENTLY
* Do you have an "issue" with alcohol or drugs?		+6	+12
		SOMETIMES	FREQUENTLY
* Do you exhibit any nervous mannerisms?		+2	+4
	EXCELLENT	ORDINARY	NOT GOOD
* What is the state of your "public" wardrobe?	−2	+1	+4
	TRIM		HEAVY
* What is your weight?	−2		+3
		SOME	CONSIDERABLE
Have you experienced any ill health in the past five years?		+2	+4
	ATTRACTIVE	ORDINARY	PROBLEMATIC
How do you rate your physical appearance?	−3	+1	+4
	TALL	AVERAGE	SHORT
What is your height?	−2	+1	+2

Your estimates . . .

*Indicates variable factor

Your Family Status, Age, and Educational Background

Factors	FULLY	MODERATELY	NOT VERY
*How supportive will your spouse be in a job search?	−3	+2	+4
	YES	SOMETIMES	NO
Does your spouse work?	−2	+1	+3
	MARRIED	DIVORCED	SINGLE
What is your marital status?	−1	+2	+4
	45 TO 54	55 TO 59	OVER 60
Are you a member of the following age groups?	+2	+3	+6
	FULLY	SO-SO	NO
Does your education match your career goals?	−2	+2	+4
	YES		NO
Did you attend a top school?	−2		+2
Your estimates . . .			

*Indicates variable factor

OPT Forecast—Total Estimates

Transfer the totals of the −'s and +'s from each category to the boxes below:

Category

	−'s	+'s
Your Situation		
Your Style and Attitude		
Your (Job-seeking) Abilities		
Your Career History		
Your Health and Appearance		
Your Family Status, Age, and Educational Background		

−'s	+'s

NET ESTIMATE

OPT Forecast—"Net Estimate"

Your "Net Estimate" represents the number of weeks you can expect to consume in a search for a job—given the present status of the factors you have rated in the categories of: Your Situation, Your Style and Attitude, Your (Job-seeking) Abilities, Your Career History, Your Health and Appearance, and Your Family Status, Age and Educational Background.

Understand that the "Net Estimate" can be *improved.* Look at how you rated the variable factors(*). These are variable in that the time listed can be decreased with remedial effort. For example, in the category of Your Situation, if your work sheet looks like the following . . .

Factors		SOMEWHAT	VERY MUCH
* If you have been terminated, how traumatic has it been for you?		+2 ←	(+4)
		POSSIBLY	YES
* Do you harbor a "hidden agenda"?	←	(+3)	+6
	YES	MAYBE	NO
* Do you have access to "networks" and are you willing to use them?	−4	+1 ←	(+5)

. . . then you can with strength of purpose and will do the following: (1) depersonalize your termination and thereby reduce the "trauma" you are experiencing; (2) get rid of your "hidden agendas" so that your energies will be fully available for a productive job-search effort; and (3) get over the possible embarrassment of an imposed job search and be willing to utilize "networking" . . . your gain can be a reduction of nine weeks.

It is possible to achieve a "− Net Estimate." If this happens, you are to be congratulated. The − Forecast indicates that nothing significant exists among the many factors to cause your job search to be any longer than it takes you to get organized, under way, and into fruitful discussions and negotiations about an offer, usually about six weeks.

Be aware, however, that the variable factors (*) can get worse, as well as the example of how they can be improved. In other words, your initial − estimate could erode, causing time to pass in your actual experience beyond what should have been expected.

Again, if you have a "− Net Estimate," or a low "+" one, follow the following guidelines from experience:

Net Estimate
+8–0 or
−1 to −20   Plan a minimum search time of two months.

Over −20   Chances are that you will be perceived as an excel-
                  lent candidate for many opportunities and that
                  very little, if anything, will stand in the way of you
                  succeeding in a search of minimum time (allow six
                  weeks).

It is worth pointing out that although we are usually right in our OPT prediction, it is possible to beat the odds. We told one client with a finance background, for example, that in our estimation it would take him six months to find a new job. Panic ensued. He told us that he had severance support for only three months.

It was clear that an all-out effort was going to be called for. First, he had to control his feelings of anxiety and panic and get on with things. Our client couldn't afford to act out *any* negative behavior—he had to do everything that he could possibly do and do it right. But remember that 37 percent of all OPT factors are within the job seeker's control. He changed what could be changed, attacked his search with energy and a positive attitude, and found an appropriate position within three months.

Immutable Factors

Now that you have completed your OPT forecast, let us discuss the categories in greater detail. Perhaps this exercise will help you to pinpoint those traits that will add time to your search.

Situation of the job seeker.   What sort of severance package did you receive? If it was *too* generous, you may feel like a poor-little-rich kid, with a false sense of security; if not generous enough, anger often prevents one from settling down to the day-in, day-out process of

finding new employment. Don't let anger diminish your efficiency—
it's counterproductive.

Be aware that if your severance package has been too generous, it
may sap your energy and ambition.

One of our clients, Frederick Sullivan, had worked for an old-line,
paternalistic corporation and had been given two *years'* severance
pay when reorganization forced them to let him go after fourteen
years.

For the first six months Fred behaved as if he were on vacation—
after all, two years' severance is a lot of money, and there was still
plenty of time left. But his approach to his job search was more than
leisurely, and consisted mostly of lunches with old chums. A few
opportunities surfaced and recruiters dangled a few jobs—but Fred
wasn't quite ready, nor was he hungry enough to bite.

Eventually, with the two years almost up, Fred had to settle for a
position that was far less interesting than many possibilities that he
just hadn't been ready for. We think that he would have shaped up
much earlier if his cushion hadn't been quite so fat and comfortable.

Are you a member of a minority group? Are you a woman, or a
representative of a racial minority? Unfortunately, everyone is not
created equal on the job-search trail, and the reality is that this will
add time. (Satisfying the Equal Employment Opportunity Commis-
sion and affirmative action requirements is not looked upon with the
same commitment that it was several years ago.)

*Do you have access to a viable network of friends and colleagues to
give you support, advice, and information about possible jobs?*
Obviously, if you do, this will subtract time. It is not considered
good form in all subcultures to ask for help, however; perhaps there's
something in your makeup that makes you feel uncomfortable asking
for a favor.

Are you interested in a career change? If you are, this will take time
to investigate, make credible to yourself and others, and achieve.

What is the ratio of your salary to your age? The "quick ratio" used
by executive search people is that if your last salary was three times
your age, then you're a "fast-tracker." In their minds, this makes you
a highly desirable candidate for a company (i.e., "Someone else found
them this valuable.")

Have you been stationed outside the United States?   Some employees return from three years in South Africa to discover that their company is closing the office there, and that they're expendable. Obviously, for these people, their networks are in disarray and must be refurbished. It will take time for them to become reacclimated to U.S. society and corporate ways.

Your career history?   Whatever you have accomplished, for good or bad, up to this point cannot be changed. See these elements as the interviewer might see them, so that you can be prepared with an explanation if necessary.

How long did you work for your last employer, and how many corporations or institutions have you been with during your career?   It is sometimes seen as a negative to have worked for one company for too many years, or indeed to have worked for one company only, particularly if it is a small company. It is also more difficult to go from a smaller company to a much larger one unless you have highly specialized skills.

How long were you in your last position?   For you to be perceived as a "fast-tracker," you would have been promoted approximately every three to five years. If you spent more than eight years at your last level, your career has already peaked.

Are you in a declining industry?   If you've always worked for companies that lease oil-drilling equipment, you will, today, have to add time to your OPT score. Clearly, there will be few jobs at your level, and it might be time for you to think about applying your skills to a more vital sector of the economy.

Are you state-of-the-art yourself and you can prove it?   Have you kept up to date in your field by either training on the job or outside courses? Perhaps the nature of your job shows that you're on the cutting edge of new technology or techniques. And if your job is actually involved with the application of the most advanced technology in your industry, then you probably will have little trouble in securing another position.

Keep in mind that it is always vital to keep up with developments in your field. If you're behind, it will show. At the very least, you should not neglect conferences (especially if they're attended by fellow industry executives—if it's worth their time, it's worth your time), nor your trade journals. This seems an obvious point, but executives often complain that they never have time to keep up with their reading. In health care, it can become a matter of life and death if those in the profession fall behind in learning new techniques, and it might be true for you, too—your professional life or death. If you have only a shallow awareness of the trends in your own industry, that's going to become woefully apparent during a conversation with an interviewer.

Your track record?   Even if you've been fired—and there can be myriad, easily understood reasons for that—it will be a plus if you can demonstrate a winning track record, whether it's in advertising, manufacturing, or general administration. If you have been a success story, it should be easy to document. If your record isn't up to date, then take time to make it so—and catch up with a faster-starting competitor in the job marketplace later.

Ideally, your résumé should show steady progression through the ranks, with each new job bringing additional responsibilities. If it does not, it will take time in your written and verbal presentation to present an alternate view.

How were you fired?   If the parting was traumatic, it is best to make valiant efforts at self-control before you set out on a round of interviews. Don't complain, as a negative attitude is going to be the kiss of death in any interview. First of all, no one much cares about the particulars of why and how. There are as many reasons as there are terminations. Second, self-righteous explanations, blame aimed at the previous employer, and self-pity is going to sit very ill with the person who is interviewing you: this year, you're bad-mouthing your previous employer; two years down the road, and you could be saying the same things about this corporation should they be foolish enough to hire you. No one wants the blow-by-blow of how rotten your employer was to you, except possibly your spouse, and you should probably hang on to your dignity with that person as well. After all, if your previous employer really did you in, and your potential employer is interested in you and cares enough to find out about the details, they will discover them easily enough without the telling tales.

Are you middle or top management? If you're already near the top of the pyramid, you have a better chance at continuing your climb than if you are still among the crowd at the middle. As the pyramid continues to change shape during the next decade, it is not the spire at the top that will be eliminated, it is the middle section, which is getting to look more and more moth-eaten. And as middle-management jobs are eliminated, the pool of possible opportunities for middle managers evaporates.

Family/age/education? This triad is the sum of what you have made of your life outside your professional world.

Are you married? If you are, this is a plus. Insurance companies are aware that married people are healthier and live longer; employers feel that such employees are more stable. If you've *been* married and have children, or perhaps are a female, single head-of-household, this will all be seen in a more positive light than having always been single. However the fabric of corporate life has changed, companies still look for evidence that a candidate is capable of making a commitment. Single people, rightly or wrongly, may be seen as too independent and footloose. And we suspect that companies are becoming reluctant to accept the responsibility for someone who signals that the potential employer will become "their whole life." With the United States divorce rate running very high, being "formerly married" no longer bears the stigma it once did.

Is your spouse working? This is considered to be a plus, as your personal confidence will tend to be higher—and confidence is attractive. Also, a spouse who is in the work force will be better able to understand the reality of the reemployment process, and also to be more sympathetic about the causes that led to your termination or decision to leave on your own initiative.

Are you over forty? If so, you may be self-conscious about your age, and women tend to be even more so than men in our present-day workplace. Understand that things are changing in the corporate and institutional world. Small companies in particular are glad to find executives who bring with them experience, and prejudice about hiring the older executive is decreasing. This will hold true as the pool of new employees entering the work force continues to shrink into the new decade.

You will, however, have a problem if you see yourself as too old to compete any longer. If you can't relax about your age and see it as a possible asset, your anxiety will add time to your job hunt.

It is still an advantage to have a degree from a prestigious school. What sort of degree depends on your field. In academe, a Ph.D. in your subject is usually necessary, and you'll get more attention if this degree is from the University of Chicago rather than a state school. In business, an M.B.A. from Harvard, Stanford, and other elite institutions is still an important credential for entry into the top corporations.

But even in the world of top degrees, perceptions change. Currently there is debate about the value of *any* M.B.A., no matter what the reputation of the school that awards it.

Corporations and institutions complain that products of even the top-tier business schools show little imagination. Some human resources departments are beginning to prefer new hires with liberal arts backgrounds—at the graduate school level as well as undergraduate—or are raiding the law firms for young people who have been practicing for a year or two.

Our moral: In your job search, do not presuppose that any part of your background is a negative and do not be apologetic. You never know when your six years in city government administration is going to strike someone as just the experience that they are looking for. They might, for example, be involved in bidding for an important contract and *you* know how to speak the language.

People may take you at your own evaluation. Although we don't advise you to emulate the saccharine child stars of films as they smiled their way through heart-breaking situations, forever seeing the bright side of life, you must project interest, awareness, and energy. This is a simplistic point, but one that is key to your making a good connection with an interviewer. It is simple cause and effect. If you do not, you will appear ineffectual and will not be considered for a second interview. Think of actors, who really do subscribe to the belief that the show must go on. A simple trick taught by counselors posits that if you continue to look cheerful, people will respond to you in a positive manner and soon you will actually feel better—even if your smile masks considerable uncertainty.

Can you project energy and enthusiasm?   If so, you will at least appear to have a positive attitude—which will make you a much more attractive candidate. Although we discussed techniques for overcoming depression in Chapter III, please note that we are not negating the real anger and anxiety that most people feel when they have been fired—or put on the shelf. But once the initial shock has faded, and you have gotten your job search started, and perhaps have even set up a few interviews, the best way to keep that positive attitude in place is to focus on your many accomplishments and to remind yourself of the contribution you are capable of making—and that some organization is undoubtedly seeking at this very moment.

Something that strikes you as negative may not seem so to an interviewer, but just in case it does, be prepared to discuss whatever it is in an open, nondefensive way. Sometimes the explanation shows real strength of character. You never finished college? Perhaps your father became ill and you had to leave to help support the family.

Or perhaps you've been in the same job for a little too long. There may be special circumstances: for example, you work for a small company and there isn't anybody else who speaks German, so you have been in the same job because they depend on you to deal with the overseas suppliers.

Or if you have the feeling that you're coming across to the interviewer as a staid middle manager without any pizzazz or energy, you might try to work into the conversation your extracurricular hobby of flying a small plane.

In sum, we advise three steps in dealing with those things that you cannot change on your résumé that you think might strike others negatively.

1. Do not dwell on them in your own mind and do not mention them first to the interviewer; do not apologize.

2. Realize that within a declining company, you accomplished some tasks that were very well executed and kept the decline from being more extreme.

3. The *quid pro quo* approach: try to balance any perceived deficiency with a positive explanation—for example, even though the company went into Chapter 11, your own department maintained its assets better than the others. If you use this technique, remember not to boast. Straightforward, self-effacing narrative is best.

Variable Factors

Several categories in our OPT predictor contain mostly elements that *can* be changed—in the areas of attitude, abilities, and appearance. In some cases, the factors that you think are negatives will have to be worked on over time—for example, it is too late to change your last employer's view of your frustration tolerance—but in general, these are traits that you can work on right away—and reap the benefits of these changes as you start your job hunt.

You might want to go over the elements in this section on variable factors with a close friend or spouse—someone who knows you well. You are certainly capable yourself of trying to estimate whether your lack of an advanced degree is going to hold you back in an organization, but when we get into the area of physical attributes and styles of personalities, you are perhaps not able to make a useful estimate of your own strengths and weaknesses. Even Snow White's wicked stepmother didn't trust her own opinion and needed reassurance as she asked, "Mirror, mirror, on the wall . . ."

As you think about the factors listed below, try to put yourself in the place of your previous employer. If asked, what would that person say about your skills or lack of same? Be candid, do not make excuses. If you think that *others* perceive you in a negative way in any of these areas—if you've noticed that you've gotten quite a lot of critical feedback—don't ignore the signals. If you can't figure out yourself how you might have gone wrong, ask a colleague, even if the answer might be painful. You really have to know the truth if you've been making the same mistakes again and again.

Style and attitude.   People are capable of establishing better personal relationships and can make enormous professional strides if they are able to modify their behavior—sometimes in small ways. But in order to gain, you have to know *what* to change.

Your management style.   Whatever report a potential employer receives from your previous colleagues about this may have a lot to do with whether or not you will be hired. If you're a "maverick" or an "autocrat," you will have made waves in a previous job but probably not have earned the devotion of your staff. Most employers prefer a more "democratic" consensus style of managing. If you're used to running roughshod over your team, and have had trouble gaining their loyalty, you should consider how an alternative way could be more productive and popular—and be ready to offer it as your expected goal in a new environment.

Do you think you're decisive? What's more important, have your superiors ever criticized your ability to make decisions? If you've noticed that your people have not in the past looked to you automatically for leadership, it might be time to consider why—and maybe remedy it with some assertiveness training.

Do you have a nine-to-five mentality? It may be that you've never been able to make a real commitment and simply cannot make any kind of extra effort. Unless you're extraordinarily brilliant, you'd better find a nondemanding job and not establish an expensive lifestyle.

Are you a high-energy type? On the other hand, if you're naturally committed and energetic, cultivate that feeling of well-being. Treat your energy supply like a precious commodity, keep in good physical shape, and don't lose your enthusiasm even during the enervating days of a job search. Vitality is very attractive—try to maintain a good energy level during callback interviews.

Are you confident in both business and social situations? We hope that you can tell the difference between an easy manner and self-centered arrogance. The latter will put off an interviewer immediately. If you haven't a clue as to what effect you have on people, this is one area in which it is worth the possible pain to ask someone who cares about you for the truth.

Of course you may find that you are one of those fortunate people who have "presence." There is no way to teach presence; you recognize it when you see it. These are people who assume that others will take them seriously because they have faith in their own abilities and have a strong sense of self that they can translate into effective action. It's the result of being comfortable with the way one is.

But if you find out, because you asked, that you do occasionally rub people the wrong way, or that you're considered arrogant, think about your personal relationships. Have you changed friends frequently over the years, and have you had one or more marriages or live-in arrangements that didn't last? Do you have children, and if so, what is your relationship with them like? If you can see that the pattern of your social life has gone awry for a very long time, we would suggest that you seek professional counseling of some sort.

Are you sophisticated? A certain amount of this is a definite plus. You don't want to appear vulgar in accent, choice of words, appearance. On the other hand, if you're being interviewed for a job as sales manager for an upstate region, there is no point in appearing too elegant during your interview, even if your last job was in the Paris office—and your French, German and Italian are admirable and your suits and shoes were handmade in Florence, which you'd probably better not refer to as "Firenze." You want to fit into the corporate culture of the moment and you don't want the interviewer to feel that you've been around perhaps a little *too* much.

You've got to know the territory. One client of ours recalls how a friend lost out by appearing for an interview for a marketing management spot in a three-piece suit only to find that everyone else was in jeans and bedecked with gold chains—it was a magazine devoted to *hard rock!*

Are you shy and withdrawn, or do you have an outgoing personality? If you are socially awkward, you will possibly make the interviewer quite uncomfortable, and if the potential job has anything at all to do with people—which it probably does unless you're a researcher or do something physical, like professional sky-writing—your inability to keep up your end of a social exchange will weigh against you. If you are at a loss for words, try to think of the interviewer as a new friend whom you don't know very well yet—remember that he or she may be feeling awkward by now, too. In extreme cases, a public speaking course, torment though it might be, will make a one-on-one conversation seem like child's play. You have to assess how your shyness is affecting your career possibilities.

Are you perceived as a "team player"? There are several aspects of your behavior at work that any potential employer is going to try to find out about from previous coworkers. If they have already discovered that your management style is along preferred "democratic" lines, then they will also no doubt discover that you were a team player.

In a Swain & Swain survey of corporate executives, the value attributed to this kind of worker was considerable. Employers want people who will show loyalty to them, will follow standard organizational procedure, and will be more concerned with getting the job done right than constantly being aware of how they're "doing," and how fast they can move up.

Society has, in the past few years, put such inordinately high value on getting ahead, making a *lot* of money, and reaching a pinnacle of success before middle age that top management is beginning to see some rather self-serving middle managers, who move along to another company as soon as a better job is offered to them. They eventually leave a trail of ill will behind them, and as time goes on they run out of good recommendations as well as new corporations anxious for their services.

How do you behave under stress?   This might be the stress encountered in a previous job or the stress of job hunting itself. If you've been cool under fire, and a previous employer passes that information along, that will be a plus in the job search. If, however, your present sense of stress closes your energy supply down, then time must by definition be added to your anticipated job search.

What is your frustration threshold?   Your tolerance for frustration—in this case the frustration of going through what sometimes proves to be a lengthy and troublesome process as you hunt for a job—is measured in the same way as your behavior under stress. Both have to do with your ability to handle a difficult situation in an adult way, as you keep going until your goal is reached—until you have a new job.

It may be that you blow up under pressure at work, and it also may be that this is not a fact about you that an interviewer will discover—but you will know this about yourself. It's a trait that can be overcome only by self-control. It may be that your personality is such that you should only work in environments that are low key, as some people never do learn to deal with pressure effectively. If, however, you love the field you're in, and it *is* high pressure, once again we recommend professional counseling, as you can learn techniques that can modify volatile behavior.

What is your mental outlook?   Have you overcome the initial depression of finding yourself out of work with no place to go? Or are you still paralyzed with shock and pessimistic about your future, as well as bitter toward your previous employer? You can learn to bring a more upbeat point of view into an interview if you do feel this way—Chapter III gives you some techniques to help you to escape from a stultifying sense of failure.

Are your expectations realistic?   Having nothing to do with information that an interviewer might glean from a previous boss, but having everything to do with your actually getting a new job, are your own expectations. You may have decided that this is the time that the perfect job is going to fall into your lap—but the position that you have in mind would really be more suitable for Lee Iacocca. You should hold on to a sense of reality even though your feelings are hurt and you want to "show 'em." A miracle is not going to happen—you are not going to get a dream job for which you're unqualified; you're going to get a job that is appropriate for someone on your level with your background. This is the time to get rid of any "hidden agendas" that you might be harboring. These are wishful-thinking sorts of irrationalities: your old company will take you back, or you'll get even in some Borgia-like way. If you don't get rid of this pointless emotional baggage, it can add months to your job search.

Your Abilities

If you have a clear idea of your real abilities, and if your work and educational background, and perhaps your personal references, support your own opinion, then you should have little trouble putting your assets to work. All of the following skills will be called on not only in a job situation but also in the job hunt itself.

For example, both in and out of a work setting your ability to focus on what's important and the skill with which you prioritize tasks are vital. We needn't go into detail about these skills—if you have them, you know it: you use them every minute of every day, including the time preparing dinner for guests or organizing the annual camping trip or getting the family out of the house in the morning. You know what to do when and what to do first. When you make a list—whether at home or office—it's a realistic list, and you try to get through it in the time allotted.

Are you able to make a valid assessment of your corporate social skills? Do you have the cluster of traits that demonstrates the ability to get along effectively in an office environment? If you have, then your record will show, for example, that you know how to "manage up"—not only do you work well with your own team, but you have established good relationships with your superiors.

There are countless ways to "get along" in the office—to achieve the liking and respect of your colleagues. Those who are most successful in carving out a smooth career path for themselves are not only competent and creative, but also are possessed of excellent communications techniques. Few people develop them automatically, but such skills can be learned—by reading, observing how others behave, even taking courses in writing or speech-making.

Good communicators do three things well: talk, write, and listen. In Chapter II, we discussed the importance of learning to write and to speak effectively. Listening is vital, too. Everyone in an office situation has something to say that they consider important, whether it is a subordinate or a superior doing the talking.

Good communicators learn how to achieve several basic goals of management. They find out that there is a problem; they talk and listen (the elements of a real conversation); they form an opinion as to what the characteristics of the problem are; they have a good enough relationship with a cross-section of the staff so that they can get a rounded picture; they decide on a solution and often, because they can present their thoughts clearly in meetings and memos, can get their ideas implemented. They are also skilled negotiators, so if there is a difference of opinion, they can work with those who disagree to achieve consensus.

Does the above profile describe you and your skills? If it does then you are among those who have lost a job through none of your own doing. You will receive glowing reports from previous employers, and no doubt will receive a viable offer.

But what if you know that the report that will be received by an interviewer will describe only mediocre communications skills, although you may be an able manager in other ways. You cannot change your personality in a moment—it may be that you will never be the most impressive speaker at a conference, or that your memos will not sing; but you *can* learn to pay better attention to your staff—it is a compliment that they will appreciate, and you may find that your department's teamwork improves as your staff gets an opportunity to "manage up."

Your Health and Appearance

It must be assumed that by now you have well-formed ideas on style, and also your own approach to health. There are no two subjects that we can think of, including religion and politics, about which more has been written or to which more attention has been paid. There are health gurus, M.D.'s, Jane Fonda, and others who have developed exercising into an art; experts on jogging, skiing, bicycling, walking; there is not one inch of the body that someone has not written about or lectured about for the lay public. In addition to your philosophy of fitness and its value to you, you may have chronic or recurrent problems; you may be a diabetic, or have a bad back; or perhaps a disabling physical problem makes the logistics of your daily round complicated. Whatever your special case, by now you have a routine to deal with your familiar physical quirks, as well as your exercise regimen or lack of same. Remember, good health is not an accident, and the resulting energy from physical well-being can only help reduce the time of a job search—and its absence will only add time.

If you've been wrapped up in the ebbing and flowing fads and styles surrounding good-health movements as well as fashion trends, then there really may be nothing that we can tell you that's new. But just in case you've been working an eighty-hour week at your law firm, or your idea of a healthful snack is a box of chocolate chip cookies, we would like to summarize a few truths about health and appearance as they specifically relate to you and the work environment—as well as the specifics of your job search.

If you have had health problems, be honest with a prospective employer. But if you can demonstrate that it has not interfered with your performance, and you can reassure them that you are not a high risk, the job opportunity may still be there for you.

*   *   *

We have in the 1980s added to the destructive properties of alcohol abuse those of drug addiction—both have become extremely serious problems in the workplace. From our observation of the managerial class in the areas of the country that we serve, we estimate that as high as 50 percent of all executives may use drugs—either cocaine or other less widely used substances—habitually or from time to time, and a minimum of 10 percent have a problem with alcohol. This is the single most critical factor in our OPT formula—abuse of either drugs or alcohol may have lost you your job, although you may not be aware of it; it may prevent you from launching an effective job campaign; and if your reputation goes before you, your drug or alcohol involvement may seriously impede your being hired, although you may have a record of achievement.

We at Swain & Swain wish that corporations could uncover drug and alcohol abusers sooner than they do; indeed, sometimes they remain undetected. But when these terminated individuals end up in outplacement, we can often identify an abuser, as this client goes through the motions of a job search with no real enthusiasm, hope, or efficiency. We can introduce the executive addict to various programs if they are willing to confront their behavior, but many will continue to practice denial and will not be helped. They can only help themselves.

There are many local and national organizations to help, from Alcoholics Anonymous to Narcotics Anonymous to church groups. If you're not willing to bring your doctor into the picture, information is available from the community services department of your local hospital—there are a lot of helpful organizations and therapists who are trained in helping you get back on track. You have to take the initiative.

Let us stress again: of all the negatives that can work against you in a job search, evidence of substance abuse is the most powerful.

There are several factors that make up a person's appearance, and if after a hard-eyed look in the mirror—from every angle—you don't like what you see, you can improve on *every* feature except your height.

Yes, people *will* notice if you measure in at extremes, but by now you may have learned the best way to deal with any new person: stand up straight—especially if you're a tall woman and have a tendency to slouch—and meet the interviewer's gaze directly, even if you have to look up.

Attractive people do better in job searches than do unattractive people—it's a fact of life. We will discuss below some negatives that you might be able to change if you feel that people just don't respond to you in the way that they do to others whom they perceive as being more appealing.

First, it might help if you had a critique of your performance in a practice interview. This is a technique that we use at Swain & Swain. It is the best way to see yourself as others see you, and a very good method of picking up odd and perhaps off-putting mannerisms, both in speech and gesture.

You'll need the help of another friend or colleague to play the role of the interviewer. Try to make the play as realistic as possible: think of it as docudrama. Go through the routine of telling a little about yourself, and what sort of job you're looking for, and some questions about the company. Talk long enough so that you feel comfortable with the exercise and are relaxed enough to be natural. Do you find that you have nervous tics? Or that you say, "You know . . ." in every sentence? Do you keep pulling up your socks or do you twist a ring on your little finger as you speak? Do you gaze blankly into space when the other person is talking? Know about these mannerisms now, before you face a person who has a real job to offer.

Have you had a weight problem ever since you were twelve, or perhaps you haven't gotten around to taking off those ten pounds that came with your latest child? As we pointed out earlier, in our discussion about self-assessment, we have found that being overweight is a very strong negative. There are some people who have a serious problem, are grossly overweight, and may have attendant health and emotional problems. That's a different business, and these people may have been trying to do something about those pounds for years—this is a problem that requires the help of a doctor and a good deal of time to do it right. Weight Watchers or Overeaters Anonymous have helped many who respond to careful monitoring.

But if you're a person who gains, loses, gains, the same ten pounds over and over, this is definitely the time to lose them. Go on whatever diet works best for you and accompany it with an exercise program, preferably one that gets you out of the house—either to a health club or running outdoors or swimming at a local pool. This will not only help your general appearance and firm up your muscles as you lose weight, but will help to offset some of the depression and lethargy that you might feel during your job search.

Try to interact with others as you go through your exercise routine at the health club, the jogging path, or the squash court. It's another glorious opportunity for that all-important networking.

Put on your most appropriate interview clothes and look at yourself in a full-length mirror. Try to see yourself as a stranger might. Do you think you measure up?

Your general appearance should be one of confident energy. Hold your head and shoulders up when you walk and be sure your handshake is firm. You will, of course, be clean, neat, and up-to-date: clothes pressed, shoes polished, with no rundown heels.

During the job-hunting process be sure that you always have cleaned and pressed clothes ready to put on. For women, this also means plenty of pantyhose on hand. When you're in a hurry, you don't want to have to rush out of the house with a run and then try to find your shade in the local supermarket. Think like a fireman. You never know when you will have to be ready for a last-minute meeting or interview.

As you start your job hunt, critique your wardrobe—women and men alike. If you don't have at least two reasonably up-to-date, completely coordinated outfits, you ought to consider investing a little time and money in obtaining at least two good suits or dresses for interviews. Although there are exceptions, in most fields "conservative" is a watchword, in everything from suit material to jewelry.

If you are a man, and work in corporate America, as do many of our clients, and have a subliminal feeling that you've been doing something wrong, go to the best men's clothing store in town and look at the customers.

You will probably see them in navy blue or dark gray or subdued wool or wool-blend suits, pinstripe or plain; long-sleeved shirts (preferably cotton) that are pastel or white (*never, ever* wear a short-sleeved shirt for business); and striped or neatly patterned silk ties. Shoes will be black or dark brown, wingtip or plain-toe lace-up styles, or, in big-city areas, tassled, fringed, or penny loafers.

There are three trouble spots in a man's outfit that have to do with length: too little of it. Vests, trousers, and socks can be too short.

Suits that may have fit when you bought them, through the mysteries of dry-cleaning may have shrunk, leaving your trouser cuffs sitting at your ankle bone. Those cuffs do not belong there, but should break over the shoe top and cover the back of the shoe by about three-quarters of an inch; vests, if you wear them, should cover your belt comfortably; and *never* wear any kind of sock that does not pull up over the calf. Pretend that your shin is the most private part of your body—no one should ever see it in the course of the business day. Showing skin as your legs are crossed in an interview has cost candidates the offer they wanted and felt qualified for, according to many recruiters we know. And, another tip, don't wear the favorite tie that unfortunately is stained dark at the point of the knot.

Although you could go into your own city's equivalent of Brooks Brothers or Paul Stuart and come out with a wardrobe that would be perfect in any upscale office, do pay some attention to your special situation.

The herding instinct is strong in human beings. On a very simple level, people feel most comfortable with others like themselves. In most companies, the top executives dress like each other, and are probably following the sartorial lead of the CEO.

Pay attention to the corporate culture of the company that you want to work for. It will have a dress code, even if unstated. You're just going to have to look around you to see what the majority of top-level executives are wearing. For starters, look at the executives pictured in the annual report. You will, of course, usually find a few mavericks— those, for example, who insist on wearing cowboy boots with business suits because they were in Tucson once and liked the way it looked.

Remember regional differences, which are very pronounced. In a popular guide to men's clothing called *Dress for Success*, author John T. Malloy points out that New York elitist pinstripe garb is unpopular in the south, where bright colors are much more common; three-piece suits are not worn much in small-town America; and bankers from Philadelphia—one of this nation's most conservative cities— dress in a bizarre, gaudy way for reasons that not even Mr. Molloy's researchers could figure out.

We discussed the question of regional wardrobes with a colleague, a New York–based national sales manager for one of the country's largest paper manufacturers. He said that he had a special wardrobe for his visits to his regional managers in the midwest. "In New York, I usually wear a three-piece pinstripe," he told us. "But my people would feel very uncomfortable if I showed up like that in Des Moines. I have a nice selection of tan suits, which I wear with white shirts and solid or plaid tics—I don't like clothes like that too much, but I look like one of the guys."

Even though women can be more varied than men in their dress, there are a few basic shibboleths that should be followed:

First, forget the look popular a few years ago of man tailored suit and shirt and floppy tie. It was never very flattering, and if you wear it these days it will brand you as an insecure parvenue.

Although you don't want to look like a man, there are certain guidelines that you should pick up from them.

Most important, be conservative. Conservative is comforting to business people, particularly men, who will make up a large part of the group that has available jobs. Another tip from the men's shops: everything should be of good quality—not only your basic suit or dress, but also shoes and briefcase, which should always be of excellent-quality leather.

Your raincoat, by the way, does not have to ape the man's. Although his should never stray from tan cotton—and that would be okay for you too—you could use a color that would complement your outfit.

A word about fur coats. In researching this book, we talked with women in different parts of the country about the suitability of wearing a fur coat in a business situation. We got so many different kinds of answers that we're just going to leave that decision up to your good judgment. But . . .

Don't wear any kind of fur coat *ever* that came from an endangered species—you're going to horrify a lot of people. Don't wear fur in areas where there may be serious financial concerns—oil and farm states, among others. And don't wear fur when there will be a lot of lower-echelon women—a union meeting, for example—who will not have them.

On the other hand, women *do* wear fur coats in world-class cities; if they're dealing with Europeans; and if they're executives in any of the financial centers like New York, where apparently the first thing that managers in financial institutions do when they can afford it is to buy a mink—and wear it everywhere. But in general your good manners and astute reading of a local situation will have to be your guide.

What kind of conservative dress or suit should you be wearing?

- Cut is more important than color or fabric. A jacketed suit or a long-sleeved dress or dress with a jacket, worn with pantyhose and either low- or high-heeled shoes, is all standard business wear. You may indulge in personal taste in color and fabric, which may be bright but not garish, patterned but not mesmerizing. Materials should not crease too easily—linen, for example, could have a small amount of synthetic in the blend—and should be of good quality so that the clothing holds its line.

- Your business clothes should not be sexy—no décolletage, nothing see-through, no *very* short miniskirts no matter how young you are, nothing that clings. Unless you are in fashion or the arts, fields in which more marked individual style is expected, don't go overboard with colors that are too bright, or patterns that are too pronounced.

- Jewelry: simple and unobtrusive. It doesn't have to be expensive; it should never clank.

A lot has been written about body language, and your interviewer has probably read those books—so pay attention to what you're telling him or her unconsciously. You don't want to give anything away until you're ready.

Three of our clients, Robert, Steven, and Kate all had the same—unknown to them—problem that was damaging during an interview: how much space to give someone in a meeting.

Robert and Steven "crowded" people, and in so doing made interviewers uncomfortable. They stood too close, held their handshakes too long, and actually moved their chairs as close as possible whenever they could. Kate, on the other hand, was quite shy, and held back physically when meeting people during her job campaign. In these encounters, interviewers felt that Kate didn't trust them, as she unwittingly projected her feelings onto them.

As you see, not too close and not too far—be aware of distance and its implication.

During the interview, observe the body language of the interviewer. Is this a friendly, open person? Establish eye contact, smile occasionally, and always look pleasant. Remember: crossed arms indicate closed thinking, defensiveness, or hostility; a cradled chin, boredom; if your interviewer has crossed his or her ankles, something is being held back; clenched hands—anxiety or anger. You should avoid these positions and hope that you don't see your interviewer in any of the hostile poses.

What Tips the Scale on Hiring Decisions?

Very Positive
  Trim/Vigorous
  Team Player
  Active in Outside Organizations

  Positive
    Married, with Children
    Humorous
    Handsome/Attractive
    Worked for Big Companies
    Tall

    Neutral
      Single
      Married, Two-Career Family
      Short
      Independent/Autonomous
      Divorced
      Worked for One Company Only

      Negative
        Worked for Small Companies Only
        Worked for More than Three Companies
        Quiet/Reflective

        Very Negative
          Uneven Career Path
          Overweight

A Swain & Swain Survey

There is only one way to sit during an interview: almost upright, leaning slightly forward in an attentive way. Don't relax too much, as you don't want to miss a syllable of this conversation.

When you speak, do so with energy. Enunciate. Southerners, for example, can barely understand the New Yorker's rapid-fire delivery. If you miss a question, ask your interviewer to repeat it. You want to project an image of awareness and intelligence.

If as you go through the interviewing process you see things in yourself that you'd like to change, remember that you have time to do it. A job hunt is an ongoing process. There is, of course, a point to it—the end result, which is new employment—but you will get much more out of the search if you learn as you go. Any process can be a dynamic learning experience—and your job hunt can fit into this useful category.

Chapter V

What Do You Want? Getting in Touch with Number One

Adversity (n.)—the state in which a man most easily becomes acquainted with himself, being especially free from admirers then.—Samuel Johnson

IN place of reading this chapter, we could instead have told you to go off to the spot where you think most clearly—a tranquil pond, a museum courtyard, your patio or deck—and make a list of everything you've ever wanted to do or have in your life, both professionally and personally, that you didn't already have.

After pruning the list to absolute necessities, you would consult with yourself and your significant others and decide what you were willing to do—to sacrifice—to obtain your hearts' desire. You would then pack up all your goods and family members and household pets and go obtain it.

But like most things in life, there's usually more to think about than can be settled in an hour or two by the side of any pond. You probably have responsibilities. And perhaps financial concerns—it may be that your job is on the line or you've already lost it. And you're not even sure that you know what your hearts' desire is.

Not everyone who reads this book will be at one of life's crossroads, but we're going to assume that you're among those who are.

You may be at the stage in life where you have to decide whether to keep treading the familiar path or change direction and gamble.

If you have recently lost your job, you might have a little breathing space, but you will have to decide rather quickly whether to return to the corporate world that you're most familiar with or delve into something new for you. You may never have another or better chance.

We cannot force you to think. But we assume that your cognitive powers are sufficiently developed so that you can come to a decision.

Let us borrow the model of thesis, antithesis, and synthesis and view it as beginning, middle, and end—the end being a conclusion. You should consider:

- What have you been and done up to this point; in other words; who are you?

- What would you like to be and do in the future; do you want to change who you are?

- If you want to introduce some fundamental change in your life, do you have any idea how to go about it?

It helps to do your thinking with a pencil and paper. Make lists, and try to get in touch with how you really feel about your worklife.

How can you find out who you are—in the sense of your identity as a working person—and who you might like to be? It is not the purpose of this chapter to tell you how to fulfill these dreams—we're just trying to steer you in the direction of possible future wish fulfillment.

A Self-Assessment

This self-assessment has been helpful to countless individuals during the past ten years who ask such questions as: "Is my style appropriate for my chosen field?" "Am I a round peg in a square hole?" "Do you sense anything in me that will cause difficulties in my next job?" "What's wrong with me? I can't seem to fit in."

As you will see, each assessment situation starts with an incomplete sentence followed by different endings. You are to distribute 10 points among the three endings to show how frequently you react in each of the three ways. Always assign a total of 10 points. Never use more than 10 or fewer than 10. You may use zeros, if appropriate, as in this example:

I usually gain the most for myself by being . . .

| 3 | friendly and outgoing. | 7 | alert to all opportunities. | 0 | careful as to what I commit to. |

In the example, the person feels that "I usually gain the most for myself by being *alert to all opportunities*" is the case 70 percent of the time, while "I usually gain the most for myself by being *friendly and outgoing*" is true for the remaining 30 percent of the time. And this person would never experience "I usually gain the most for myself by being *careful as to what I commit to*," hence the 0 in box three.

A note for you: Consider the statements in a work context and don't labor over your choices. You should be able to complete the assessment well within ten minutes.

After completing Part One, total the columns. The sums of A, B, and C should add up to 100. With that done, continue to Part Two. In this section, you will see that the statements deal with adverse situations. Again, answer quickly, with your first reactions. Remember, there is no right or wrong.

PART ONE

	A	**B**	**C**

1. I enjoy things most when I am . . .

   [ ] helping others do what they want   [ ] getting others to do what I want   [ ] doing what I want.

2. Most of the time I am apt to be . . .

   [ ] quick to respond to the needs of others   [ ] energetic and quick to see opportunities   [ ] careful and not rush into things.

3. When I first meet people I am most apt to be . . .

   [ ] concerned whether I will be liked   [ ] curious about them   [ ] polite, but cautious.

4. Most of the time I find myself being the one that . . .

   [ ] others can count on   [ ] supplies the direction   [ ] studies things before acting.

5. I feel most satisfied when . . .

   [ ] major decisions have been made by others   [ ] others count on me to make major decisions   [ ] I've had time to study a decision.

6. People see me as a person who can be counted on . . .

   [ ] to be trusting and loyal   [ ] to be full of ambition and initiative   [ ] to be unswerving in my convictions.

7. It is most like me to . . .

   [ ] do the best I can and trust others for recognition   [ ] take lead in developing opportunities   [ ] be patient and practical.

8. I would describe myself as one who is most often . . .

   [ ] friendly and open   [ ] energetic and self-confident   [ ] cautious and fair.

9. I find relationships most gratifying where I can be . . .

   [ ] of support to a strong leader   [ ] the one who provides the leadership   [ ] free to pursue my own way.

10. When I am at my best, I most enjoy . . .

    [ ] seeing others benefit from my help   [ ] having others turn to me   [ ] being my own boss.

Totals

[ ]   [ ]   [ ]

PART TWO

A	B	C

11. When opposed, I am most apt to . . .

☐ put my wants aside to be helpful   ☐ become forceful and push on   ☐ become more cautious.

12. If I want to overcome opposition, I will try to . . .

☐ change to become more acceptable   ☐ find holes in others' arguments   ☐ appeal to sense of fair play.

13. In getting along with difficult people, I usually . . .

☐ find it easier to go along for the moment   ☐ find them as challenges to overcome   ☐ insist on equal respect.

14. When someone strongly disagrees with me, I tend to . . .

☐ give in and do it their way   ☐ challenge and argue   ☐ detach myself from the situation.

15. When someone openly opposes me, I usually . . .

☐ give in for sake of harmony   ☐ battle it out   ☐ try to withdraw and turn to other interests.

16. If I'm not getting what I want from a relationship, I am most apt to . . .

☐ keep hoping that things will work out   ☐ become more forceful and push harder   ☐ look elsewhere for what I want.

17. When I feel others are taking advantage of my good will, I usually . . .

☐ ask for advice of those with more experience   ☐ fight for what I feel I'm entitled   ☐ state my rights and insist they be respected.

18. When another person insists on having his own way, I tend to . . .

☐ put my wishes aside for the moment   ☐ counter argue and try to get him to change   ☐ respect his right if there is no interference with mine.

19. When someone openly criticizes, I am most apt to . . .

☐ want to pacify the person   ☐ challenge the criticism   ☐ become more cautious.

20. When someone has plainly abused my trust and confidence, I tend to. . .

☐ feel they have harmed themselves more than me   ☐ get angry   ☐ analyze what went wrong.

Totals

☐   ☐   ☐

Transfer your totals to the following graphs:

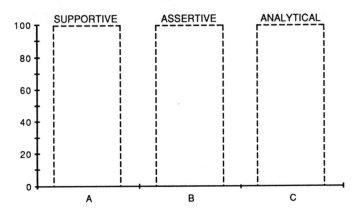

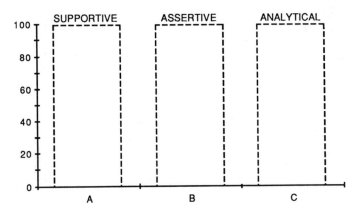

Your profile will emerge by drawing solid lines to indicate the height of each column and then by "cross-hatching" the space below. For example:

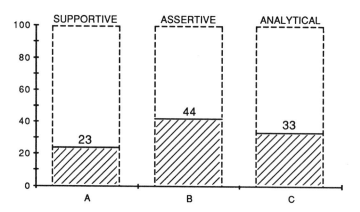

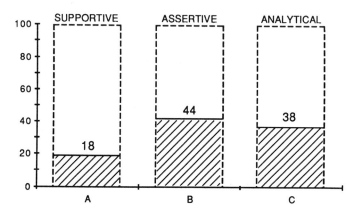

This example demonstrates the typical profile of a line-type (versus staff-type) person. In each column, you have an indication of how the person's energies are directed under favorable and unfavorable conditions. From experience, we can share with you a whole range of descriptive profiles. See whether, or how closely, your own profile matches these examples. The implications of each are provided.

Line-Type Person

Appropriately assertive, accustomed to leading. Is analytical before being supportive.

Under "attack" will stand firm and become even more analytical.

Staff-Type Person

Appropriately supportive and analytical. Takes reflective pleasure from company's success.

Under "attack" remains clear-headed without giving up supportive quality.

The Start-Up Leader

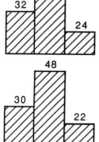

Full of enthusiasm for the "idea" or "venture"— doesn't hold back for second thoughts.

Adversity only causes renewed assertiveness.

The Planner

The mind always keeps working—not distracted by emotion.

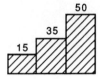

The Hot-Head

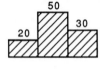

Assertiveness run amok. Often charged with "overreacting."

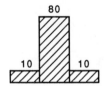

Paper Tiger

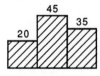

First seen as fairly assertive, sometimes hard-headed.

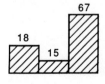

Under resistance or adversity, gives way and withdraws into being "analytical."

Mixed Message

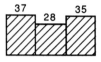

First seen as "on the team" as long as things go well (or their way).

Under adversity, forgets to be "supportive" and instead becomes highly assertive (even hostile).

The Mystery Person

The overall impression is one without definition—flat.

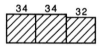

People usually wonder how to read or motivate this type.

The Bleeding Heart

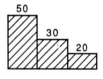

It's all too evident how "supportive" this person is.

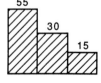

Despite adversity, the person "holds on." Usually rewarded with being called "stubborn"—this is not a compliment.

Obviously, some of these profiles are unflattering and probably troublesome. If you sense that your own profile falls into this category, we recommend that you explore any of the behavior modification programs that are generally available (often at modest cost).

While your profile cannot be either right or wrong, it may suggest that you have been miscast:

(1) in a line role when you should be a staff person,

(2) in a start-up role when you are the longer-term visionary that should remain in planning, or

(3) in a staff role when clearly you have line-officer energies.

Who Are You Now? Your Accomplishments and Shortfalls

We suggest that you think first about what you know you're good at— your area of professional expertise. Has your work given you job satisfaction and some measure of creativity or self-expression? Or are you often left with a flat feeling—boredom—or, worse, are you under constant stress because of an impossible office situation that you don't seem able to change?

Think about whether your skills—which are the result of on-the-job training, background and education, talent—have been well utilized. Add in character traits and personality—are they all suited to your work environment?

We have noticed in our assessments at Swain & Swain that when a man is asked "Who are you?," he has a tendency to answer along the lines of "I'm a marketing executive," or "I'm a portfolio manager"— even if that was his last job and he has just lost it.

Women, on the other hand, are quick to see themselves in the broader sense, as in: "I am an active person who copes with the demands of a career and family," or "I really like working for a bank." They are able to view themselves as many-faceted personalities. If men see themselves that way, they are not usually able to talk about it.

This is a fine opportunity not only to review the categories in which you have been successful, but to actually measure any satisfaction that you have received from that success—or even from the process of doing a job that may not have ended too well. It's sometimes hard to be honest with oneself. You may have a job with an international bank, with responsibilities for a think-tank operation that predicts the economy of the world in the year 2000. You make a lot of money and the prestige is all you dreamed of when you were getting your Ph.D. in economics. But now, after your eighth year, you grimace when you think of having to go to Paris for yet another meeting.

This is a sign of stress. Please see Chapter VI, "Stress Awareness: Tune In," that will point out that you may not be as contented as you think you are. It might, for example, be time to leave the fast track and try to get a staff-support job.

It is surprisingly difficult to figure out if you're doing what you ought to be doing. The stress of literally not having ten tranquil minutes during a workweek to spend with your family—and maybe not much more time on a weekend as you suit up even on Sunday to spend a few hours in your office—precludes your being able to think about much in an abstract way.

So if you're between jobs now, take advantage of this found time to examine the details of your day-to-day work life as you've known it. This is a quality of life assessment. How has yours been up to now? Be honest with yourself. You will accomplish very little if you tell yourself what you think you *ought* to want to hear.

Appearances mean nothing if you're not happy with the reality beneath the facade. If you really don't want to be in the helping professions, for example, don't force yourself to go in that direction. It's your life. Face up to your real interests—we would assume a certain bedrock of ethical behavior—even if they seem quirky to others.

YOUR PHYSICAL ENVIRONMENT: If your pulse accelerates when you realize that the corner office with the wraparound windows and the wall-to-wall carpeting and the Chippendale side chair is really yours, then you should recognize that status symbols are important to you. You don't have to admit to anyone that the more buttons your phone has the better you like it, but do admit it to yourself.

This does not make you a shallow person who doesn't give to charitable causes, but it does make you the sort of person who should not accept a job for a shirt-sleeve, old-fashioned manufacturing company in the warehouse district of town.

But you should ask yourself whether you're not too preoccupied with perks and comforts when you think about the pros and cons of a job. Remember that today, as the super corporations downsize, there is a greater chance that you will find something suitable with a smaller, less grandly appointed company or institution. Don't give up an interesting opportunity because there is no executive washroom.

Perhaps you should focus on *why* the externals are so important to you. It may be that your job with a world-class corporation was your first introduction to a sophisticated world of travel, hotels, and restaurants. The experience of ordering a limo and charging it to Mega Corp.—not to mention your company American Express card—can be very heady if you're not used to it.

But traveling first class on airplanes, and all the trimmings that used to go with it, are becoming a thing of the past—it doesn't have much to do with job content anyway, except possibly to point up that you have to go to the head office in Denver a lot. Realize that most of the goodies are only toys; they're fun, but maybe it's time to look beyond these things.

YOUR COWORKERS: The corporate culture—or institutional ambience—generally determines the sort of employee who stays and thrives. The ones who don't fit in move on eventually.

This doesn't necessarily mean that in one company the employees are all similar in appearance and outlook, although you do find that in some corporations, where, for example, a middle manager would rather be drawn and quartered than show up at the office in a light-colored suit.

The corporate or institutional culture *can* be one of openness and individual expression. There are, after all, differences among individuals, and although many of you are employed by what we consider "corporate America" and do wear pinstripes and blue shirts with white collars à la Lee Iacocca, many of you may be used to theatrical management companies or interior design firms, or have been involved with organizing traveling art shows or industrial photography.

People in fields that can claim even a tenuous relationship to the arts often take their individuality seriously—that's *their* corporate culture—and work very hard to establish a style that is theirs alone.

We know of an actor who throughout his twenty-year career has prided himself on showing up for auditions and rehearsals in banker's gray with whatever power tie is popular at the moment. He carries his makeup in a leather briefcase from Crouch & Fitzgerald that any

CEO would be proud to own. No jeans and T-shirts for him. His idea of suitable work clothes just happens to coincide with the standard view at Merrill Lynch.

Have you, in the past, given high priority to your relationships at an office? Even if you have, your interaction can take many different forms.

You may be the sort of person who makes a friend every time you pick up clothes at the cleaner's. Or you and your wife still have dinner with that nice couple whom you met in Barbados four years ago.

Obviously, you have a warm and open personality and friends are very important to you. Your management style is predictably democratic and you've no doubt developed close friendships with people on many levels in your corporation from top management down through the members of your staff.

That doesn't mean that you can only flourish in an open, "creative" atmosphere. You may be much more comfortable working for a traditional manufacturer, for example, but your job should be people-oriented and there ought to be a lot of interaction and openness between the managerial levels. You would not do well in the kind of corporation where every in-house communication is transmitted through desk-top computers.

Perhaps you reserve real intimacy for family and friends outside the work situation. Even if this is true, do you at least have good working relations with your coworkers? Do you know a little about their families, and do you occasionally have lunch with some of them?

This is the usual, quite comfortable, semi-social office situation. You know your coworkers somewhat but don't necessarily share a summer beach house.

But close relationship of another kind can be based on your passion for work. You and your coworkers may comprise a fiercely dedicated team—involved, say, in R&D at a major cosmetics company. You may all be mesmerized by the challenge of completing an especially difficult project.

Each team member is an equal partner, each gives maximum effort. You all thrive on hard work, deadlines, follow-through, and successful solutions. You're most comfortable with other people who automatically coalesce to form a cohesive, can-do team.

If you're happy in this sort of atmosphere, you should look for another position that is project-oriented, with a corporation where the employees have a reputation for working very hard. You're a team player and a workaholic—a valuable combination from the company's point of view. There are lots of others with the same combination of traits and you will probably find a place on one of their teams.

Not everyone is an even-tempered team player. Not everyone has good interpersonal skills, or likes to manage a department, or wants to do his or her tasks in a group environment.

The stereotype of this sort of person is the creative loner—the computer expert who sits alone with the machines and programs and figures out where all the glitches are. These people do exist, and fit within the category of productive introverts.

But there are also plenty of you who have some trouble relating to your staff and colleagues and yet do not have the luxury of retreating to an ivory tower and still making a living. You may have had difficulties with management in the past and your personality might even be the reason that you were fired from your last job.

And yet you—and previous employers—know that you have a lot of talent.

What sort of work environment would make best use of your technical expertise and yet put you in a milieu that you can deal with successfully?

Don't work for the sort of company in which there is a lot of client contact—a service company, for example.   You will do far better in an organization where they make something—like paper or nuts and bolts. You are task-oriented.

Don't accept a position in which you will be responsible for trainees.   Work with an experienced staff. You may be impatient, quick to criticize when a task is not done to your specifications and perhaps intolerant if a team member doesn't catch on right away. You are at your best working with other specialists.

But the point of this chapter is for you to figure out what makes you happy. If you find it truly impossible in an office situation, and perhaps have lost jobs because of your irascibility; if you walk around with a knot in your stomach each day, and your temper is ready to explode, it may be time for you to think about professional counseling in stress awareness and management.

THE CONTENT OF YOUR JOB: There are two points to consider when you analyze jobs that you've had: did you find them satisfying at the time, and did they make good use of your skills and talents? Obviously, if you answer yes when thinking about past employment, you're going to try to duplicate your previous experiences.

Clearly, jobs are undesirable if they don't address positively the points on the following list, but your work situation could be considered satisfying if:

- You have enough autonomy to create, implement, and complete a project.

- You have a staff that is experienced enough to implement tasks under your direction and to whom you can delegate real responsibility when necessary.

- You have a voice in setting goals for your department. You are present at all meetings that have to do with your team, and your input is important.

- Your projects are realistically planned and although you are expected to work hard, you do not have to be at the office every night and every weekend. Some allowance is made for a personal life.

- You have real responsibility for your staff—you have an important say in hiring and firing, raises and promotions.

- You plan your own budget.

- You can hire your own support staff.

- Your relationship with your boss is workable. You don't always agree, but he or she is willing to listen, and you have always found support forthcoming in dealing with top management.

- You do real work—not just manage a staff or write reports about what other people are doing. Your job has content—whether it's seeing that the automobiles roll off the production line or the magazine gets on press or your client's speech is in her hands before plane time—what you do is real.

- Your work has something to do with your talents. If you're a whiz at numbers, then you're in accounting or computers; "Mr. Charm," then you've always been involved with public relations or account management firms. Most important, you're doing what comes naturally and you like it.

If you *haven't* been liking it, it's very important for you to recognize that now. It often appears to us that the world is full of people who spend every day in their offices excruciatingly bored. These are the people who would love to leave their chosen or assumed fields. Some know exactly what they'd like to do and some just know that it better be something very different from what they've been doing. But it's very hard to give up all that training and professional equity that have taken years to acquire.

Only you can decide how badly you want to make a change. A lot depends on your family situation, and available resources. But remember that sometimes it's possible to translate your talents into another language. An attorney who's tired of corporate law but is fascinated with the theatre could open a practice specializing in show business clientele. It means a gamble, but it's not starting from square one.

THE CORPORATE AMBIENCE: What sort of environment do you feel most comfortable in?

As we've mentioned earlier, there are fewer jobs available with the international grand masters of business and finance, but there are plenty of middle-sized companies and institutions that are organized on traditional, hierarchical lines.

You may feel most comfortable in a semi-military atmosphere, where everyone works toward clear goals and the lines of command are well drawn. You may have an autocratic management style, and not be very flexible, but on the other hand you're efficient and a good problem-solver and completely loyal. You just don't want to wing it managerially; you need to have every goal clearly delineated.

There are naturally almost as many styles of company management as there are corporations and institutions. Some are small, some middle-sized, some grand; family-run and public companies; non-profits and educational institutions. Some may be democratically ruled and some in an oppressive autocratic style.

Some elements of corporate culture that others admire may leave you cold—you may not want predictability—and yet you might be perfectly happy in the sort of company that most others would avoid as a matter of course—for example, most employees don't want to be subject to frequent erratic shifts in corporate goals disseminated by a less than competent top management. But you might have the personality of a rebel—you thrive on crisis and change. You have also learned that in a very volatile corporation, the chances of you being promoted unexpectedly because someone has quit in a rage are at least possible.

Only you can decide if you want action or stability. But, once again, be honest with yourself. By now you should be enough in touch with your own likes and dislikes to know whether you like a challenge or a sure thing; intellectual stimulation or the stimulation of working in a group. There must be many work environments that would feel like home to you.

YOUR SHORTFALLS: Have you reached the point at which you can learn from your mistakes and management failures?

Have you been listening when your work and behavior have been critiqued in the past by management? Do you have deep-seated personality issues that you don't understand very well yourself, but which drive management crazy—and for which you've recently been fired?

Disassociate yourself from your own frustration and anger and isolate the strains of criticism that you've heard again and again.

Management problems.   Although you don't like to face the truth, you have over the years probably heard the same complaints from your supervisors.

- You are not a team player. You're not interested enough in the success of the group—and by extension, the project—but only in the credit you'll get for your contribution.

- You are an indecisive manager. This may occur more often if you're a woman. Women still face a great deal of prejudice in corporate America—your supervisor may not want you to climb any higher on the corporate ladder or you may indeed be an indecisive manager. As we've mentioned earlier, women receive substandard training in managerial techniques for the most part. They have to learn by doing, a situation that will certainly improve as more women move into middle- and top-executive ranks.

  The key to becoming decisive is to keep your goal, whatever it is, firmly in mind. If, for example, you schedule a project and it's due on a certain date, check up on it at a midpoint to make sure that it's properly in the works. You should have planning meetings at which your staff reports on progress; they should understand that unless extenuating circumstances have arisen in the interim, a planned due date is firm. If it's one of your top priorities, and you're vocal about it, it will become a top priority with your staff.

- You don't listen to your staff.

  Think back to your premanagerial days, when you were new to any kind of work situation. Everything that affected you—a change in job title, a new boss—was of fascination and importance to you. So it is for your staff.

If they have a conference with you, everything they tell you is important to them, and they will listen carefully to the way you respond.

Pay attention, because you are the manager and responsible for your staff. You have the power to aid their careers or block them, so you must not treat this power lightly. If any one of them has a complaint, you should know about it. It may not be too important to you, but a good manager will keep every stratum of his or her department running as smoothly as possible.

· You don't do enough information sharing. If your staff is going to perform at peak efficiency, they have to know a lot of what you learn in the course of your job.

Information sharing takes a lot of time, perhaps time that you feel could be more profitably employed in getting through your paperwork, but it is your job to inform, and train, and even nurture your people. If you don't, you deserve to be criticized.

· You don't manage up well.

Your superiors may feel that you're working in a vacuum. They want to know what's going on in your department and you haven't bothered to send them as much as a half-page memo.

Keep them informed about successes as well as difficulties, which they're going to find out about anyway. Write memos, schedule short meetings with your boss. Don't be a mystery guest at the office. If they don't know what you do, and how you're doing it, you will surely be one of the first to go during any kind of reorganization.

Personality issues.   We want to list a few failings that one would *think* you would be fully aware of if they were part of your personality and character. But denial, especially with disturbed, anxious, stressed, neurotic—or, more seriously, unpleasant, bullying, dangerously erratic—individuals sometimes is the *only* reaction.

Some people can always excuse away failure or criticism: his boss had it in for him because he was jealous; it wasn't her fault that she spoke sharply to her secretary—the computer had just made a mistake; that new person is just too sensitive and can't take a little well-meant criticism.

But the reality may be that:

· You have an alcohol-dependency problem and your temper shreds when you haven't had a drink for a while—right before five is an especially hard time for you.

- You have deep-seated feelings of insecurity and love to pick on those more vulnerable than you. You're a bully.

- You are too ambitious. Your ruthless tactics are clear for all to see. Your coworkers are not as blind as you seem to think.

- You're not as well equipped for your job as you and management thought at the beginning. You're over your head and instead of asking for help you're blaming others for your failures. Your team dislikes you.

- You're chicken-hearted and can't deal with real trouble. Under stress, you abrogate all responsibility and leave the pieces for others to pick up.

- You're insensitive. You don't listen and don't really empathize with others.

- You're not especially trustworthy. You make promises—it could be about anything from a raise to a vacation—and then, through indifference or unwillingness to stick your neck out, you forget all about it. Members of your team ask for transfers a lot.

- You're jealous. You never delegate any job that you don't absolutely have to, and you seldom give any member of your team credit for a job well done.

- You're lazy. You delegate everything you possibly can get away with and expect your staff to work unto exhaustion. You, on the other hand, try to get off right after lunch on Fridays so you can get your sailboat in the water. This behavior does not go unnoticed.

- You're just plain bad-tempered. You've been indulged as a child and as an adult and the result is that you have got to have things just your way. You have no idea of behavioral boundaries.

Do the villains of these pieces ever recognize themselves? Or do they think that a little irritability is to be expected and that everyone loses his or her temper from time to time?

And when does someone finally seek professional help? There has to have been some productive self-examination along the way. The individual perhaps will recognize that there is a problem with interpersonal relations but does not have a clue how to alleviate them. Recognition is half the battle—it might even be that the person can modify his or her own behavior up to a point.

But anyone who is very angry for a large part of the day ought to do something about it—the best way being to get to the sources of the anger with the help of a counselor.

THE PROFESSIONAL ASSESSORS: If you think that you might want to try new employment avenues, yet self-assessment is a skill that eludes you, there are for-profit organizations, as well as community programs, that assess clients' personality, aptitude, and interests.

You might be the sort of person who is interested in what the experts think—if you are, it might be helpful for you to seek out one of these organizations in your area.

Dr. Harold Weinstein, a vice-president of Caliper Human Strategies Consulting, Inc., a human resources consulting firm, has said that "it's very difficult to engage in self-assessment," going on to point out that not only do companies like Caliper offer assessment for job seekers, but also community colleges and organizations like the New York City Federation Employment and Guidance Service and the Catholic Charities.

What might you expect if you consult with one of these organizations? You will no doubt speak with a counselor, and fill out questionnaires of varying length and complexity, and, if you have consulted one of the private companies, will receive a personality evaluation that will indicate your strengths, perceived weaknesses, and interests.

These tests and their results are never scientifically accurate to the same degree necessary for a mathematical theorem, but they are reviewed according to standard psychological analysis and should at least tell the client how his or her interests and reactions translate into predictable behavior. This can be very helpful in trying to figure out what went wrong on the last job or what sort of organization one might be happy with.

Let us give you an example of the sort of results you might expect:

One well-known company that helps management motivate their employees is Kahler Communications, of Little Rock, Arkansas. The avowed aim of the Kahler questionnaire is to have each employee gain self-awareness in order to change his or her own work-related behavior if it's counterproductive—a pattern of repeated failure in some area, for example, or a lack of maximum effort in another.

The results of the answers to the Kahler "personality inventory," places the employee in one of six personality categories—Reactor, Workaholic, Persister, Dreamer, Rebel, or Promoter. Examples of things that you might learn about yourself if you fall into the Workaholic category are:

Your character strengths:	Logical, responsible, and organized.
Facial expressions:	Furrows on the forehead (worry lines).
Traits:	Ability to think logically, take in facts and ideas and synthesize them.
Basic distress sequence:	Expects self to be perfect. Frustrated with people who don't think clearly enough.

And so on. But this can be quite helpful if the employee is incapable of engaging in any sort of self-analysis on his or her own.

At Swain & Swain, personality assessment is a very important part of what we do—we must understand what makes our clients tick if we are to suggest avenues that will be productive.

We see a lot of good guys—the ones who are:

· pragmatic

· optimistic

· realistic

· self-activated

· win-win managers

· good listeners

· know themselves and how to nurture and attract support

· don't expect instant gratification

On the other hand, there are the bad guys. We also see people who:

· have mixed agendas

· can't control their anger

· have unrealistic expectations

· have no impulse control

· are afraid to take risks

· are lazy

· are too rigid

· lack empathy

· are narcissistic

In other words, we deal with every personality and character trait that's common to the general population. Of course, the more we know about our clients, the better we are able to help them.

When a client comes to Swain & Swain, he or she speaks with our psychologists and counselors and completes a number of self-assessments. In order for us to guide the client in a helpful way, we must know about his or her values, personality, skills, and likely behavior patterns under favorable and unfavorable conditions.

VALUES: Our objective in analyzing these assessments is to match as closely as possible our client's values with the components of a potential job. Values might involve creativity, independence, helping others, freedom, recognition, security, increased knowledge, warm relationships, high earnings, tranquility, or even adventure.

There is, of course, no right or wrong answer, but we must clarify what the client's essential values are so that at least we will know which jobs are a realistic possibility.

PERSONALITY: In our assessment and interviewing in this area, we try to help the individual to understand himself or herself as well as others in the work environment. We talk about different work styles, as well as the sorts of behavior that are conducive to job success. We also try to identify and minimize potential conflicts with others— particularly if our client has had some behavioral difficulty along the way.

SKILLS: Most important of all, we need to know if the client is going to be suitable for a particular kind of role. We therefore work very hard to:

· identify all the individual's skills

· confirm stated career interests

· suggest other career possibilities, if appropriate

The point, of course, of all the above and everything else that we do at Swain & Swain is to increase our clients' personal awareness and self-confidence and guide them to the ultimate goal of self-motivating action.

Your Future Goals

We would hope that by now you know whether your career path has been satisfying or not.

It is possible that you want something more out of life than you have been able to obtain up to now. It might be:

- more money

- freedom from the nine-to-five routine

- more security

- the time and flexibility to do good work

- the chance to try something creatively satisfying

Everyone's list will be different. Are any of these goals realistic? We believe that with planning, patience, and perseverance almost anything is possible.

A psychotherapist we know spent several years as an editor for a textbook publishing company. Becoming a psychologist seemed an unattainable goal, but she took advantage of the educational benefits offered by her employer and started taking a few night courses a semester. Somehow, the credits kept piling up and by the time her company relocated and left the city in which she was living—effectively putting her out of work—she had finished her dissertation. She had only to pass the state licensing exam and hang up her shingle.

We do think that anything is possible, but it has to be realistically attainable with an investment of time and effort. You will have to tailor your plans to your own situation and resources.

We can't tell each of you how to reach an individual goal, but we can suggest general guidelines that most planners for the future should think about. This is not fantasy time; you have to be practical.

If you think that you would like a business of your own someday, just keep that goal in the back of your mind as you go through the job-hunting process.

Get yourself a job that will teach you something about the business that you want to go into and start taking courses in small business management at night.

It's never too soon to start thinking about financing your venture. Most small business people capitalize with a combination of savings, loans from relatives, and commercial loans. Talk with bankers now and learn what their requirements are—what percentage of your capital can you expect to borrow from the bank? Find out now to avoid disappointment later.

You may want to change careers or you may have to change careers— you're in a dying industry.   There is, of course, a difference between changing careers—deciding to go to law school, for instance, when you've been a men's wear buyer for years—and trying to find a managerial job like the one you had, except you would like to leave shoe manufacturing and give exercise bicycles a try.

In the latter case, persistence will probably win the day. You will eventually find a manufacturer of exercise bicycles who will give you a chance.

But when further education or training is required, as in the law school example, you have to think about the financial commitment and demand: Are you a two-career family? Do you have any children? If you do, then the salary of your spouse will probably not cover all the expenses that have needed two salaries to meet. Parents may be able to help, but that might incur a financial or emotional debt that you don't want.

Our feeling is that if you truly want the kind of career change that requires additional training or education, then you'll find a way to deal with the difficulties—and enjoy it. But make sure that your spouse wants the changes, too, because while you're learning about torts, the household chores will fall on his or her shoulders, and presumably their own jobs already fill the days adequately.

Are you in debt?   If, for example, you owe thousands to the credit card companies, you're behind in your car and house payments, your ready-credit account is overdrawn, and in addition you owe everybody in town and haven't made good on last year's Super Bowl bet, you may need professional financial counsel.

You need someone to draw up a budget for you—and maybe even make a deal with your creditors if you're in a real bind. You might think about getting some free-lance work or moonlighting at a second job, income from which will be applied only to your debt.

All your credit cards *must* be destroyed or you will never get out from under.

You must be reasonably credit-worthy if you ever want to go out on your own. You will need a good credit rating. Start on that road to solvency now.

You do, unfortunately, also have to plan for a "worst possible" scenario.　Can you really plan to move to Florida if your mother-in-law is in a nursing home in Boston and there are no other children or close relatives in the area? Whatever you were planning to do in Florida will probably have to be done in Boston unless you move the whole family with you.

You have to think about death and illness, because even if you're relatively young, if you have parents, they're going to get older—and may get sick and need care.

If you have siblings, it's best to start discussing the possibilities long before the issue comes up. You'll at least know then what's expected of you and what options remain to you in planning your future. We don't mean to be gloomy, but if you're trying to introduce more flexibility into your life, it's good to know exactly what your responsibilities are likely to be a few years down the road.

A word about money.　Some people are working as hard as they can in their area of expertise and they're not going to make any sort of quantum leap in salary in an office situation. Unless they invent something very cheap to make that everyone needs, or buy stock in the Xerox of the future, or get left a lot of money by a relative, then they're probably not going to make a great deal of money.

But all things are relative—even what is considered an attractive salary. It is possible, for example, to shift from a low-paying field like publishing or teaching and find employment with a TV network. The increase in salary, although thought nothing special by twenty-six-year-olds who have never known anything but soaring stipends, may seem like true riches to the ex-teacher or magazine editor.

You may yearn for extra time away from the office to work seriously on your photography or to tutor minority kids in reading or engage in some other volunteer work that's important to you.　If you're not rich, these are activities usually left to retirement, but if you want to try to rearrange your life now to include them, then you might not look for another corporate job but pursue our midpreneurial course of action described in Chapter X. You may have to work harder than you ever did before, but at least if you want to photograph the early-morning light on the bay you could arrange your day to accommodate it.

What universal guidelines would apply to all you readers—from different backgrounds and with disparate dreams—who want to change your lives?

(This is not, by the way, always in the direction of greater flexibility and freedom). We know many entrepreneurs and small business people—a graphic artist and an interior designer come to mind—who each during their middle years went to work for the design department of a large company. They were weary of the anxiety of drumming up new business week after week and the uncertainty of a manageable cash flow. A monthly paycheck seemed like a gift from heaven.)

Our guidelines are based on the standard instructions given to newspaper novices on how to write a lead for a newspaper story. After the first few paragraphs, the reader should always be able to answer the following: who, where, what, when, why—and so should you if you're thinking of leaving the niche that you know.

1. *Who?* Are you interested in a venture that will require partners? How will you share the costs and responsibility? Do you have these people lined up or will you have to find them through advertisements or word of mouth? Is it really a good idea to borrow money from a relative—what will that do to family dynamics?

2. *Where?* Are you planning a move to the Sun Belt to open a crafts store? Or set up as an independent accountant? If you contemplate a geographical move, check out the area with great care. Find out about housing costs and rent for commercial space and taxes—if you're going to a resort area, you may be horrified by your projected expenses.

   You can be no less careful if you're opening a store or looking for office space in an area you know well: Go to the district that you're interested in and investigate the shopping patterns. Some locations are just bad news—and no one knows why. One side of a street might have enough walk-in trade to support every store on the block—the other side of the street might be absolutely dead.

   We've all seen new restaurants open with great fanfare on a neighborhood corner—and then close six months later. Some sites are the kiss of death. Make sure that you're not stuck with such a lease. Find out the history of the location in which you're interested.

3. *What?* Have you thought through the value of your enterprise? Is this project really necessary? You have to do your own market research no matter what the enterprise.

   If you're going to set up as a consultant, for example, in an attempt to introduce some flexibility into your workweek, is there a need for your services? Does your industry use consultants as a matter of course or are you going to have to go into the marketplace and break new ground? Be realistic about whether there really is a market for your service or product or whether you're going to have to create it. If you're uncertain, if it's a gamble, don't risk everything unless you have financial support that's steady—like a spouse who works.

4. *When?* What is your time frame? Are you planning a venture that will require further education? Or do you need capital that will necessitate months or even years to raise? Are you waiting for your daughter to graduate from college to help you?

   If you do have arrangements to make over a long period of time, with very little to show for your efforts, keep your goal firmly in mind and don't become discouraged. This is where patience will become your most necessary virtue.

5. *Why?* This is the most important question and the one that only you can answer: you see a need, you want to be free from the structure of a team effort, you think you can make a better life for yourself and your family, or perhaps just because the challenge is there.

You have an excellent chance at success if you understand clearly all the details of your proposed project or plan—and set realistic, do-able, step-by-step goals.

Chapter VI

Stress Awareness: Tune In

Did you hear what the white rat said to the other white rat?. . . I've got that researcher so well trained that every time I ring the bell he brings me something to eat.—[anon.]

What Is Stress?

We hear the word "stress" everyday as part of the common catch phrases of the eighties: we're under emotional stress, we're dealing with stress in a positive way, we're stressed out. We have a tendency to view stress as a physical entity—a thing that comes from outside ourselves—but in reality stress is a state of mind, a perception.

It is true that when we think of stress we also think of all the externals that we associate with it: the part of life's difficult experiences that challenges our body to respond in the ancient fight-or-flight reaction.

But not everyone perceives life in the same way. One mother, for example, might become enraged by the sight of a brand-new fast-food restaurant in the neighborhood, with attendant rise in blood pressure, every time she drives by. Another might be delighted—it's a terrific place to bring the kids—and experiences pleasure when she sees it.

An event that bothers someone badly one day if they're depressed and tired—a lengthy visit from a boring neighbor, perhaps—may not cause a second thought if that person has had a good night's sleep and is waiting for a friend to come by for some conversation.

There are, of course, many of life's problems that are not open to stress interpretation: marital troubles, death of a loved one, loss of a job. But even the pain that we feel during life's crises ebbs in time; if there is a residue of debilitating unhappiness and anxiety, we can learn to cope with it if we understand why we feel the way we do.

We obviously cannot, in this chapter, analyze your every emotional reaction and give instructions to help you "feel better" always or to give tips so that you can eliminate all stress from your life. There are no quick fixes and you will sometimes be anxious, uncertain, unhappy—all the internalized results of stress.

We're trying in this book to give practical advice to help you get through this difficult period of displacement and reentry. We will share with you our advice to our clients—whom our consulting psychologists counsel in techniques to recognize causes of stress, which is the first step toward reduction of its symptoms—without recourse to medicine or drugs.

Stress, by definition, is a state of arousal with which the body and mind respond to demands from challenges of work, home, and play—demands that are beyond the ordinary. It is a disruption of equilibrium, which results in a condition of tension for that mind and body.

Long ago, W. H. Auden voiced his discontent in a poetic narrative set in New York, *The Age of Anxiety*—a title that has found a permanent place among the descriptive terms of this century. Today, the words are still apt.

Although anxiety is probably the permanent condition of modern humankind, abstractions are not all that helpful when one has to get through yet another trying day. Each generation sees its time as being particularly fraught with problems and anxiety producing. Each generation is right. You are probably better off, say, than the Anglo-Saxons in Great Britain at the time of the Norman Conquest, but if your job is a nightmare or if your boss is distant and aloof or if you've just been fired, historical perspective may not help. And that's just at work. Your personal life may be in discouraging disarray also.

With job uncertainty and constant effort to best increasing competition as two of the few constants in our business world, it is not surprising that the work environment has become unpredictable and frenetic.

We like the image of each person having an individual "Pac-Man." As an employee's feeling of well-being decreases, a malevolent Pac-Man runs riot, devouring a person's coping mechanisms, psychic energy, and inner strength. The more unstable your situation, the more stress you will experience, and Pac-Man will prevail.

The Effects of Stress in the Workplace

Unrelenting stress is not something that can be ignored—it can have a profound negative effect on both our behavior and our physical well-being and must be controlled, if not reduced.

Dr. Carol Wilkinson, a New York–based medical doctor who has had a corporate practice, helped us to isolate typical behavioral characteristics encountered when an employee is under too much stress.

The overstressed employee may:

· Show evidence of declining productivity. He or she may be reluctant to take on new tasks, may withdraw from the team and withhold input, in general be "not all there" during the workday.

· Start to take sick days. This employee may not show up on some days, and simply excuse it the next day by saying that he or she wasn't feeling well. The sick-day allowance is generally used up quickly. There is no real evidence of ill health. One joke goes, "He used up all his sick time and called in dead."

· Become involved in a series of accidents. These may occur either in or out of the office, and usually are the result of distraction: the employee rams the car in front of him, or spills coffee onto the boxes of paper near the copying machine.

· Miss deadlines. Work promised for a certain day simply does not appear.

· Show anger and irritability with coworkers. Be vocally unhappy with the nature of the job.

· Be newly indecisive. A competent executive may suddenly have trouble coming to a decision or giving instructions.

· Show evidence of drugs or alcohol.

These are warning signs—the result of unhappy preoccupation or substance abuse. Clearly, the underlying causes of the manifest stress will have to be uncovered and dealt with.

Dr. Wilkinson believes that 35 percent of all medical ailments have their basis in stress; in addition, stress is probably a contributing factor in *70 percent* of all physical ills.

Most medical professionals continue to err, says Dr. Wilkinson, in treating the symptoms only. If the causes of stress remain, the symptoms will very likely reoccur or find new ways and places to manifest themselves.

In a clinical setting, although some of the symptoms could have other roots, if the syndrome is present, it's generally safe to say that stress is too.

If you suffer from a combination of the symptoms below, we probably don't have to tell you that you're under a great deal of stress.

- Tension in your jaw and neck muscles

- Racing pulse

- Rising or high blood pressure

- Unexplained perspiration

- Flushed appearance

- Light-headedness

- Chills

- Shortness of breath

- Cold hands

- Trembling

If these are your symptoms, then you already know that the level of stress at which you're operating is much too high. It's bad for your health, bad for your soul, and bad for your relationships. You need to change part of your day-to-day structure. If you can't figure out yourself what in your life is especially stressful, you probably need professional help—someone to help you put into practice techniques like the ones we use at Swain & Swain, which we will discuss later in this chapter.

How We Cope with Stress

Cumulative stress, if not relieved and reduced, can in extreme cases destroy you. There are many gradations along the way, but constant stress is at the very least damaging to your career and health. We know what the symptoms can be: depression, irritability, poor job performance, impotence, failed personal relationships, aggression, anxiety, fatigue, insomnia, ill health, obesity, phobias, drug and alcohol abuse—all are possible and the list could continue.

You can learn to control the effects of stress much as you've learned other management skills. The sources for each person's state of stress are largely individual, composed of your own internal frustrations, which are in turn rooted in your life history and psychological makeup.

The coping mechanisms that you develop will be yours alone, and you are usually the one who decides what they should be.

Even though much of what we encounter in the world around us can cause us anxiety and feed our state of stress, the *cure* for stress does not lie in the external world, but rather within each of us. To be successful in overcoming the effects of stress, we should understand our personal stressors, identify the sources of them inside our minds, and learn to activate our coping remedies.

Swain & Swain's Stress Awareness Program

Bookstores and libraries contain a bewildering display of books on stress management. All sorts of methods are advocated: exercise, meditation, other relaxation techniques, diet, biofeedback—all treatments of the symptoms, not the underlying causes, of stress.

External halfway measures are not the answer—it's like painting an old boat without taking the trouble to scrape the hull first. The paint job won't last because the underlying trouble wasn't corrected.

When clients come to the Swain & Swain office for outplacement, most are under stress. They have, after all, just lost their jobs. Assessments give us some idea as to how much stress they're under, and the passage of time tells us how well they manage that stress. The results, naturally enough, differ widely—with the clients at one end of the chart remaining almost paralyzed and accomplishing absolutely nothing, and those at the other recovering quickly and getting on with business.

An outplacement firm is not in business to get a client a job—we are not a search firm. Rather, we exist to aid the client in seeing himself or herself as others do, and making sure the client is in a positive frame of mind, equipped and able to find his or her *own* job.

We are, however, above all practical. When it comes to job hunting, we follow the old adage: "If it works, do it." So although we would *like* the following scenario to be commonplace, it usually isn't so comfortably neat:

1. Client Alice comes to us for outplacement.
2. Alice is depressed—after ten years as manager of the public relations department at Mega Corp., she and her staff have been eliminated. Mega Corp. will be using an outside firm from now on to save on permanent payroll and benefits. Alice is resentful and hurt and has some harsh words to say about Mega Corp. to her counselor and the consulting psychologist.
3. By week number two, Alice has recovered from the initial shock and although still somewhat angry, has attacked her job search with enthusiasm. She liked the job she had, and is going to try to find one like it. At week's end, her log shows that she has made thirty-two phone calls and set up four luncheon meetings.
4. Week number three finds Alice in the throes of meetings, and mailing résumés to recruiters, and custom letters to others; phoning, and by Thursday she has set up two interviews.
5. Week four Alice goes to a concert and runs into her first boss—a woman whom she had called during week two—at intermission: "Oh, Alice, I was going to call you tomorrow. I think I've found just the thing for you. Call Fred Smith at . . ."
6. Week five: Alice sees Fred Smith, and Fred's boss, and . . .
7. Week six: Alice meets with the CEO of Fred's company. They're eager to hire someone just like Alice, and in fact they'd like to hire Alice . . .

Although jobs do sometimes spring up as if they were mushrooms, generally our clients have to do some creative digging. And, also, our *knowing* that a job is out there somewhere for each of them isn't enough. The client has to be in the right frame of mind to plan, to search out, to interview, to follow up, to convince.

But all that takes mental and physical energy and a certain tranquility of spirit so that you can stop worrying about yourself and concentrate on the task at hand—getting back into the work force. Some of our clients cope with their feelings of loss and find enough energy to take positive action. Some don't. They suffer from overwhelming anxiety and fear, are under constant stress, and end up only getting ready to get ready.

At Swain & Swain, we believe in self-motivation, consultant support, and direct action. We expect you to be mentally tough, but we do realize that for many of you—our clients and you, the reader—the shock of being at liberty, perhaps for the first time in your life, can be unnerving.

Recognizing that something more was needed than "Look, Roger, you've been hanging around our office now for three weeks and haven't sent out a single letter or made one phone call. Let's get this job search on the road," we developed a stress awareness program to help our clients learn to manage the internal frustrations that fuel stress, and to improve their coping mechanisms. We try to teach techniques of self-awareness, because only when we understand *why* we perceive a certain situation as stressful will we be able to change the behavior that feeds the state of stress.

In planning this program, we had the extraordinary contribution and creativity of Dr. William C. Stewart, a colleague and psychotherapist who specializes in human resource motivational training and development.

We needed to develop a model to help our clients identify sources of stress. How was that going to help?

It seemed to us that if Client Alan performed Action A fourteen times a month and all fourteen times the result was Result B, and Result B caused Alan pain and suffering, then he would stop performing Action A. The trick is for Alan to recognize what Action A is, and that it's a predictable part of his behavior pattern.

The building blocks used by a well-balanced adult to construct a life are in the areas of love and work. A successfully integrated person is one who receives gratification from both.

"Motivation is the key," says Dr. William Stewart. "We try to activate our clients or get them to self-activate."

We always hope that our clients will be able to help themselves—whether it's getting their job search started, correcting some deficiencies in appearance, or learning self-awareness. "We're not going to change the environment," says Dr. Stewart. "And that wouldn't resolve stress anyway."

To become stress-free is not realistic, but we can change the cause and effects in our own lives if we decide to make our own decisions—based on the reality that we see about us. There *are* options open to each one of us.

Some Coping Suggestions

Most of us realize that stress is a "many colored robe" and that it tends to defy popular remedies. In our view and experience, these remedies serve to strengthen only one of the available stress-coping mechanisms, namely "Self-Care."

For the sake of feeling better after what you have just experienced or may be planning to do, let's look at "self-care" and the several other coping mechanisms that we can employ. The arsenal includes:

Taking physical care of yourself—the ability to achieve a healthy body, typically the result of appropriate diet, rest, exercise, and the absence of tobacco and alcohol. The media has helped us to know this coping mechanism better than the others and, as a result, we quickly recognize the results of negative self-care practices. Good self-care gets us through the stress of career uncertainty, avoiding the garden variety of aches, pains, and flu-induced fevers.

Seeking support—the ability to share your needs with others and to make clear your interest in obtaining support or assistance. To attack stress with this coping mechanism is one of the easiest solutions to acknowledge the wisdom of and the hardest for many to do. They wrongly believe that "seeking support" will diminish them in the eyes of others, when we know that the reverse is true: people are flattered to be sought out for support and feel rejected when you don't do so. Learn to seek support directly and be receptive when it's offered.

Managing your time—the ability to make efficient use of your time as a valued resource in accomplishing your goals. The depleted condition of this coping mechanism is evidenced by disorganization and out-of-control tasks and activities. A system for managing your time requires a statement of goals, available time, and the prioritized allocation of effort to these goals and their elements.

Raising your self-esteem—the ability to recognize your own worth and to grant yourself self-respect. Clearly, our responses to events are shaped by who and what we think we are in our work and careers. Many of us "beat up" on ourselves, devaluing our own efforts and abilities. Raising your self-esteem is one of the most important routes to stress coping and, very briefly, involves learning self-acceptance and becoming free of the many things that Dr. William Stewart refers to as "items in the little red wagon we all drag along behind us."

Gaining situation mastery—the ability to respond appropriately in our work and careers, neither over- or underreacting. Career crises and transitions severely test this stress-coping mechanism and we all have first-hand experiences with the lack of situation mastery, making us "wince" at their recall. A better approach is to become more patient, develop priorities, learn to pace yourself and live each day with reasonable expectations.

Developing a positive outlook—the ability to view your work and career with an optimistic, hopeful attitude—not expecting the worst. Unfortunately, "Positive Outlook" and "Situation Mastery" seem to be the most weakened stress-coping mechanisms today. What we usually see is the reverse: the belief that things are bad and that they will not be getting better anytime soon. Developing "Positive Outlook" is the companion effort to raising your "Self-Esteem." Libraries have numerous books on both subjects; read them and learn to become hardy in the face of stress. It's really worth the effort.

Chapter VII
Making the Big Move: Mounting a Job Campaign

Job Search (n.)—a season pass on the shuttle between heaven and hell.
—[anon.]

Assess Your Marketability

It is a major adjustment to think about working somewhere else, doing something else, changing offices, colleagues, perhaps even fields.

You could be someone who opts for early retirement, or who can afford to get a mid-life graduate degree or sail a balsa raft along some ancient trade route, but chances are—unless you choose to start your own business—that you'll be looking for some kind of job at the kind of company or institution with which you are already familiar.

How will you fare against the competition? Part of the challenge of looking for a new job involves the knowledge that the process is both predictable and unpredictable. As in all kinds of relationships, you can seldom predict when the chemistry will be there—or not. You might get the job of your dreams after falling into conversation with a small-business owner in the taxi line at the airport. Anything is possible, but it does seem a good idea not to overlook traditional avenues.

We suggest that you try to see yourself as potential employers will see you. Self-assessment is difficult, but your point of view is as useful as anyone else's. At least you will be able to tell what might be within your power to change. Be candid with yourself. The point of this kind of self-examination is to try to predict what sort of first impression you might make, and how you can improve that first impression. As one sage remarked, "You don't get a second chance to make a poor impression."

Of what is a first impression composed? It's the outer you—the way you look, act, your initial materials: your résumé or letter of introduction. As you are interviewed, the potential employer will be aware of how you appear and will want to know about your educational and social background and previous job performance and experience.

HOW YOU APPEAR: It may have been quite some time since you looked at the physical you. What will the interviewer be seeing?

1. Do you look fit, or are you overweight? (We've discovered, in continuing surveys, that being too heavy is a *very* strong negative.)
2. Are you dressed in a way that is appropriate to your field and function? For example, the gold-link bracelet that might be terrific on a male show-biz attorney is a definite no-no if you're being interviewed by a Wall Street investment bank.
3. Are you absolutely well groomed—hair combed, shoes polished, accessories in good taste?
4. Is your manner easy without being too casual? Are you aware of feeling uptight? If you are, the interviewer will see it, too.
5. Are there any apparent sociocultural characteristics that negatively affect your suitability? For example, are you a woman in a male-dominated field, or a member of a minority race applying for a job in a company or institution in which white males occupy all the top management slots?
6. Do you feel too old? If you perceive yourself as being a little over the hill, then the interviewer will pick up on it. It's a plus if you appear physically vigorous, no matter what your chronological age. Also, experience has seldom enjoyed such a premium as it does now, and why not? It's only the experienced that can help a company avoid pitfalls and get jobs accomplished in less time.

YOUR BACKGROUND: You know all about different kinds of corporate culture, and you will be off and running if your background happens to fit in with what's considered desirable at the company of your choice. For example, a very different sort of person would be looking for a job as managing editor of a big city daily than would be applying to Merrill Lynch as a commodities expert. We know of one company in which *all* of the top management of the generation that is just retiring had been officers in the Navy during World War II. Foot soldiers need not apply.

Unless you are trying to enter a new field, in which case you will have to do some research, you probably have a clear notion of what a possible employer might care about.

1. Do you have the right educational background? Is a graduate degree necessary?

2. Will your personal life have anything to do with whether or not you're hired? Does it, for example, make a difference if you've been divorced? Is it a plus to be a family man, with a nonworking wife, if you're male; is it a negative to be a single, head-of-household working mother? Are you gay, and will you have to fight homophobia in the workplace?

3. Do you think that you have a real handle on the corporate culture of the company that interests you and that you really understand all the nuances of what they're looking for? Or are you aware of cultural undercurrents that you can't figure out? If you really can't tell what sort of person they're looking for, it's probably best to concentrate on a company whose corporate culture is easily understood by you. Or you may find yourself in the position of trying to figure out the shorthand conversation of a group of people who have known each other since they were three years old and their families all summered together on an island off the coast of Maine. Then, to prepare for Yale, they all went off to Andover, while you were an ice hockey hero at a large public high school in Minneapolis.

   Think of such an upper-crust firm as practicing a kind of nepotism and stay away from it. You also may not want to work for a small family-owned company that has three children working their way rapidly up through the ranks. They're going to get the interesting jobs long before you do. You will find that there are plenty of other opportunities, where promotions are based more solidly on results.

PREVIOUS JOB PERFORMANCE: How will your job history appear to the interviewer?

1. Do you have solid training in a field that is growing? In that case, you'll probably walk into a job similar to the one you just left without any difficulty.

2. On the downside, have you had too many jobs—or too few? Have you

worked for a series of small companies, and are now thinking of applying to a multinational? Your lack of international experience might hold you back.

3. What will the interviewer find out about your personality when the human resources department checks your references? Have you had a career marred by personality problems? You've never, for example, gotten along with superiors and are irascible and impatient with your staff? If you're looking for a managerial job, this sort of history will label you as unsuitable.

4. Along similar lines, what will the interviewer find out about your character? Did your previous employer think of you as a loyal employee? Are you a team player? Are your ethics beyond reproach?

5. What about your job performance? Will previous employers talk of your flexibility, and management skills, the ease with which you handled promotions, your outgoing, affable personality, your intelligence, creativity, and efficiency?

Obviously, you want a positive answer to as many of the above as possible. If you can tell immediately that there are areas in which you don't measure up, factor them into a sensible plan. Appearances can be worked on, liabilities turned to assets. There's not much you can do about your background, but what can be done is worth the effort. After all, it's *your* life, and it's unique. By now, your life history should be rich enough for you to choose positive elements from it that would be interesting to the kind of company that would interest you.

We mean for you to see the process of securing a new opportunity as a campaign in the true sense: it is a "series of well-defined and planned steps designed to bring about a particular result." The result in this case is not the conquest of northern Italy by Napoleon—it is your employment in an occupation and position that you consider worthy.

The campaign we speak of is a process, with a beginning, middle, and end, all of which will be discussed in this chapter. It is a mistake to foresee the end of the process too early on—but it can be predicted. You may think today that an acceptable conclusion can only be a position with a Wall Street firm—you don't know that the perfect role for you may be with a management consulting firm that you have not yet heard of.

Your Campaign Plan

Remember: there are *always* opportunities available, no matter what the season. If we listened to popular wisdom—"No one is hiring, it's right before Christmas," "Don't bother to look now, everyone is on vacation"—no one would ever work anywhere and there would be no point in even getting out of bed.

Because your search may be a lengthy process with the end not yet in sight, you ought to approach it as you would any important project—control it by reducing it to its parts and then . . . divide and conquer. Analyze the components and break the whole into manageable sections. There are several basic questions that you should ask yourself:

1.   Are you in the right frame of mind to begin this search?   Have you controlled your anger and resentment that you were bound to feel when you were terminated? Although you still may be feeling a little unsteady, you ought to concentrate on avoiding the highs and lows of emotional swings and learn to remain as equable as possible. It's a plus if you resurrect your sense of humor. Concentrate on showing a positive and upbeat face to the world. Your search can be, after all, an adventure.

2.   Have you managed to get in touch with your real goals—are you focused?   Do you know what kind of position you want, and do you know for whom you would like to work? Do you want to relocate? By now you probably have been in the job market long enough to know that you are at an advantage if you know exactly what you want to do and for whom you'd like to do it. If there are only a few possible companies in your field, you have done enough research on them to know what the possibilities are for employment—you're aware of their product and you may have colleagues who work there. You may also have a list of senior executives who might be interested in your work. You have looked at the relevant annual reports. And you've sensed the "open marketplace" by reading the display ads in the major newspapers.

Among the companies that you know best may be those that are in competition with your previous employer.

Eugene Wood was a product developer and market planner for a major communications company who was advised to begin his target list with the obvious choices: direct competitors.

He researched the leading competitor and identified the one operating unit where his experience related most directly. His letter of introduction was straightforward and reasonably brief (and, significantly, it traveled alone without his résumé).

Unknown to Eugene, but predictable in the sense that change is the only constant, the president of the group he had written to was wrestling with two recent developments. A company he had caused to be acquired was experiencing a decline in sales and the general manager had just resigned to take a position in another city.

The group executive had promoted the second in command (a numbers guy) in the troubled unit to be general manager and decided he needed a new product planner for the backup spot. Eugene's letter landed on his desk and seemed like a gift from heaven. They met with Eugene and were delighted.

If your goals are not quite so specific, you will at least know which of the following are important to you:

· The size of the company or institution.

· Its product, or services.

· Whether it's in the private or public sector.

· Its corporate culture and general reputation.

· If it's a growth field.

· Its location.

You will also have defined your own ideal position well enough so that you may have some idea whether it is being performed or not in your targeted company.

3. *Do you need counseling?* By this we mean professional counseling. At Swain & Swain we can offer our clients career counselors and psychologists if they're overanxious or unsure what career path to follow. If you have been fired and feel stunned and desperate several months after the event, you may have to find expert help on your own. Sometimes just a few sessions with a counselor will make you

realize that you are by no means alone and that your skills are definitely salable.

We don't mean seeking out the opinions of friends and loved ones. They may have your best interests at heart, but that is not always an advantage. They may tell you what they think you want to hear. In addition, unless a friend or relative works for a corporation that you'd be interested in joining, their information may be just guesswork or based on hearsay. You need better information. The suggestion that you be sure to contact this or that search firm is usually a direct source of disappointment—and it's no fault of the search community.

4.   Are you prepared to work hard?   A meaningful search is a real full-time job. You need to spend six hours a day on the process— indeed, your work will never be done. There are always more letters to write, thoughts to consider, directories to examine, phone calls to make, or meetings to attend.

You will be your own marketing manager, public relations expert, and administrative assistant; you're trying to market yourself and you have to keep careful control over the process.

You will have to bring all your organizational skills into play. You will keep meaningful records of whom you have spoken to, written letters to, been interviewed by. The Italians have a phrase, *bella figura*, meaning that you do things in the proper way, with style, so that no one is embarrassed. It is not *bella figura* to send two copies of the same introductory letter in the same week to the same key executive at a company that you would really like to join—keep track of what you are doing.

5.   Do you view yourself as a product or service?   As something to market? You may see yourself as a most charming fellow or woman, but potential hirers are going to see you as a product or resource— something that they may or may not invest in. It is your job to see your possible contribution as a tradeoff with your potential employer—they will pay you a salary, but in return they expect to make money. You must return more to them than they will give or they will hire someone else or no one at all. You therefore must present yourself as an attractive resource with a blend of background and training that will make you a profitable addition to their team. An employer wants a productive employee, and no doubt someone will at some time during your search offer you an appealing opportunity, but remember that any corporation—and even a nonprofit institution—wants the most they can get for each dollar. Your task will be, in part, to heighten that perception of your value to their needs. Keep that relationship in mind and what you say will not be seen as "blowing your own horn."

6. *You want to start your search with confidence.*   We hope that by this time you have recovered somewhat from the trauma of termination and are prepared to think of yourself as the skilled and experienced person your résumé represents.

We suggest that before you work up your résumé you review your career and outline your accomplishments—your contributions over the years to previous companies.

This exercise will provide a basis for your résumé, but more important, it will reinforce your sense of self-worth and focus your own ideas of what sort of position you are most qualified for—and interested in.

First outline your work history. Start at the beginning. Give dates, job description, and major responsibilities for each job. What was the departmental situation when you arrived, and what was it when you left? Were you directly responsible for positive changes? Be specific—can the results be measured? If so, put them in terms of dollars, time saved, customer relations salvaged, production increased. Remember the qualitative aspect of your work as well.

This worksheet is for your eyes only. It is helpful to list the kinds of satisfactions you got from each job—and the specific frustrations and difficulties you experienced. A pattern may emerge: it may turn out, for example, that what you enjoy most is interacting with other people. If this appears again and again in your review of previous employment, pay attention—and look for that sort of role again. On the other hand, too much close supervision of your work may have driven you crazy in numerous assignments. Take heed and recognize the probable need for a more free-wheeling organization.

When you prepare your list of accomplishments—a version of which will sometimes be sent or shown to an interviewer—try to see that list through the interviewer's eyes. He or she may not be familiar with your company: if you say something like "Increased sales of Product X threefold during first two years in new position" it really means nothing unless considered in context. Whenever you list an accomplishment, even if it sounds most impressive—"Created new software package that helped to streamline marketing operations in three warehouses on the West Coast"—you should remember that the interviewer has to know a little bit about what the accomplishment really means.

It would probably be more effective—when you get to the construction of the résumé—to list fewer accomplishments and add enough information so that the reader knows why whatever it is that you see as an accomplishment really is an important one. In the first example, that of increasing sales of Product X, it may be that an increased advertising budget for Product X coincided with your coming in as product manager. But it would be a *real* accomplishment if you had increased sales threefold with the same sales staff and budget. Give your interviewer enough specifics or your listing of accomplishments may not have much impact.

7. *Have you thought through the technical and administrative aspects of your job search?*   If you are not in outplacement, do you have an orderly place to work? And if you can't type very well, do you have access to a word processor or the help of a paid secretary or devoted friend who won't resent you after the hundredth letter is typed?

If you are no longer affiliated with a corporation or institution, you will need your own letterhead. Go to a good stationer and choose a white or cream rag-content sheet; your name and address should be in an easily readable typeface—stay away from anything convoluted like Gothic lettering. You don't want the recipient to have to guess at your name because you've been creative in your choice of typeface.

Black ink is usually best, unless there is some pressing need to be different: you're opening up shop as a consulting landscaper and you think that leaf-green ink on bark-colored paper stock will be most effective.

Avoid thermographic raised type; it was originally introduced to ape the more-expensive engraving, but instead has won a tacky reputation. It *can* be used for brochures, but we see no reason to order it for personal letterhead—plain black ink on white or cream paper will look fine and not distract the reader from your objective— to have him or her read the contents of the letter.

Go to a stationer and buy those office supplies that your company once provided from the stockroom. You're on your own now, and will need: scissors, a small postage meter (you can weigh a letter with enclosures without having to run to the post office), stamps, large manila envelopes, the usual pens and pencils, typewriter of some kind (even if you're having your correspondence retyped, you're going to want to know how it looks), typing paper, yellow pads, blank mailing labels, Scotch tape. This is an obvious list, perhaps, but you may not have thought about some of these items for years. As you begin work, other items will become necessary—such as three-by-five cards.

You may, for example, decide to keep your names, addresses, and phone numbers on index cards; you will certainly want file folders, and perhaps will invest in a file cabinet. You will learn about Express Mail and Federal Express—you're going to have to get information to interviewers overnight. Make sure that you have access to the cheapest possible telephone system that is available to you—especially if you're willing to relocate; and even if you've not used credit cards up to now you may find that it will be handy to have one available for quick trips or unexpected lunches that you think you should pay for.

8.   *Call or write to your prospective references.*   Never volunteer anyone as a reference whom you have not checked with first. It's just good planning—if nothing else it's flattering for them to be considered important to your campaign. You also might want to explain what sort of job you're looking for so that they can stress that area of your background. Your references should be your "board of directors"—those who think well of you and not only want to help you, but are savvy enough to understand what an interviewer wants to hear about you.

When you hear that a reference gave an interviewer a good report about you, be sure to call or send a thank-you letter.

9.   *We started this list talking about your frame of mind and we'd like to end with another comment about attitude.*

As we've mentioned before, but it cannot be stressed enough, *you* are the product, and *you* have to market yourself. If you don't approach the process with enthusiasm and a sense of coming success, then an interviewer will see you as an unknown or uncertain resource. If that happens, you've presented yourself ill-prepared, or to the wrong audience.

You not only have to appear positive on the outside, but if you are to be successful you have to feel as positive on the inside, too. A search may take several months. Properly done with an appropriate spirit, you'll actually begin to feel better and more secure in your abilities each day—much like the major league pitcher in July after a shaky start in the spring. But you have to keep at it every day; you have to make phone calls and write letters and set up appointments every day—and some days, when nothing at all is happening, you're not going to want to bother. After all, what possible difference could a day make?

Well, a day is the invasion of Normandy, and a day is the day you got married, and a day could be the day that you happen to call the right person—someone whose marketing manager has just decided to move to Norway and go into the salmon business, and your résumé looks pretty good.

You don't have to put in an eighty-hour week. But you do have to look upon your search as a real job—and put in normal working hours.

Don't allow yourself to be discouraged at the outset. Compare your first effort to spring training. The beginning weeks will be spent testing and getting your résumé in order and writing some letters. As time goes on, and you have made many phone calls, and sent out many well-thought-out letters, and talked to numerous people you know and many that they know, you will begin to enjoy the rewards of such effort: awareness of numerous opportunities and the pleasure of being considered for them. A well-organized search will have a ripple effect—but you have to throw in the stone and follow the ripples. It takes a while for the ripples to spread. But X may pass your résumé on to Z, who had heard of you from T, who thinks you are pretty good in your field. So Z will call you for an interview. All this takes time, but it produces quality results.

As we have said elsewhere, a good technique with which to battle any tendency to passive behavior is to set small, obtainable goals for yourself. If you look at your log for a week and see that you made forty-one phone calls, you can predict that in the coming weeks you will come into view of the final results you seek.

First Impressions: Your Résumé and Letters

Whole industries have been created in attempts to teach the job seeker how to formulate the perfect résumé—the one that will stand out from the rest and convince the prospective employer that his search is over. But in reality it doesn't work that way—so many books have been written about how to construct the perfect résumé, and so many "résumé consultants" have set up shop, that many of the results are beginning to look overprocessed, "canned." Employers are beginning to complain of too many fanfares and furbelows—they no longer can tell from some résumés anything about the candidate and would like to see a return to basics.

We agree—and would like you to think "simplicity" when you write your résumé. It is a starting point in your job search, and it is the minimum price of admission to be taken seriously in a search. You may also think of the résumé as a business card—it is something to leave behind after a meeting to act as a memory aid for the person whom you've just spoken with.

A few years ago Swain & Swain conducted a survey in which we approached more than five hundred hiring executives across the country. In an attempt to discover more about ongoing corporate hiring practices, we uncovered some strong opinions on the value of résumés—and opinions about their content.

A significant percentage of the respondents thought that job seekers invest too much time and energy in formulating their résumés. They thought that they were in fact more important to the job seeker than to the prospective employer. About 42 percent felt that executives could probably manage just as well without a résumé, relying on letters alone, and one respondent thought that a solution would be "to produce résumés only in face-to-face meetings."

According to the survey, an unsolicited résumé signaled to 51 percent of the respondents that the sender is unemployed and is perhaps sending his or her résumé to every corporation in town. It is, of course, okay to include a résumé with an exploratory letter, but we've found that the letter—if you explain your objectives clearly—is often enough.

The same guidelines that apply to all your written communications apply to résumés: they should be clear and they should be brief.

1. Quality. Let us take as given that you will have it done professionally by a competent typist and printer. It should be on decent-quality bond, photo-offset rather than photocopied, with good spacing and adequate margins. You must proofread it yourself—and get someone to check you.

2.   *Length.*   One page is best. The person to whom you're sending it gets hundreds of résumés in a year and does not want to read about your experiences the way only your parents might.

At Swain & Swain we recommend a flexible two-pager. Page one contains your positioning statement: who you are, what you've done, where you've worked, your education, and basic personal information.

Page two summarizes your accomplishments. We recommend a series of detailed vignettes that highlight your greatest successes and give a good idea of your strengths and experience.

In a way, each entry must *prove* your claims to an interviewer.

Allan Stern, managing director of the executive search firm Haskell & Stern, has told us how important it is in a résumé to be specific: "If an applicant says that he was responsible for increasing profits by 100 percent, then he must support that statement with hard data in a clear and concise way."

We think that a detailed second page—with a few main entries—is the proper place to give that data.

3.   *Content.*   We've discussed page two above. This is the interpretive section—his or her accomplishments as seen through the eyes of the job seeker—and should be either sent or given to the interviewer when appropriate, during an interview, for example.

Page one is the outline of your career—with entries chosen, naturally, to put you in the most favorable light.

It will contain basic data: your name, address, phone number.

In addition, it encapsulates your work experience. There is a convenient way to arrange this information: in chronological order, allowing the reader to scan the page and feel reassured that he or she is facing someone appropriate for the need at hand.

A chronological listing shows a nice progression up through the ranks, with increasing responsibility. Human resources people prefer this type of listing, because it gives them a good idea of exactly where you were when.

The respondents to the Swain & Swain survey felt that although job seekers may have spent too much time worrying about their résumés, they spent not nearly enough thinking clearly about the purposes of the letter that accompanied the résumés (or could have come by itself).

The letters received by the respondents, they felt overwhelmingly, were too general—no one wants to get a letter addressed "Dear Executive"; too effusive—one middle manager did not think that he deserved the title of "Industry Leader"; self-aggrandizing—"I think I can turn around your small appliances division based on my history of can-do aggressive management"; or just plain vague yet self-serving—"I'm looking for an opportunity to further my personal growth."

In general, many of the letters, the respondents felt, were presumptuous demands for help, were quick to tell the reader what the letter writer thought he or she needed, and almost utterly self-serving—with very little if any mention of what advantage it could possibly be to the reader to help this person.

But there is no reason why letters, sent with a résumé, or letters of introduction, or letters seeking information have to be offensive, or pointless, or a waste of time. On the contrary, we think that they're a vital element in your job campaign: you use them to position yourself in the market. They're your method of announcing that you are available and capable.

In advising our clients on content, we recommend the following:

· Be clear. State the reason for writing and have only a limited number of objectives in each letter. You are writing to clarify your purpose in getting in touch with the recipient.

· Be explicit. Keep your letter simple so that the reader understands immediately what you want.

· Be brief. If you're not, no one will finish reading it.

· Use short paragraphs. A great many busy executives are not going to read every word in every letter, especially when it's not related to the business at hand. If you confine one thought to one paragraph, your reader should have no trouble understanding what it is that you're asking. You want to avoid confusion.

· Never threaten. Do not indicate in any way that the reader owes you a favor, even if he or she does.

Letters of introduction are written to four different categories of individuals:

· People you know, and have had some sort of ongoing relationship with—they may be friends or colleagues;

· People with whom you have had some previous relationship but haven't heard from in a long while—a previous boss might fall into this group;

· People whose names you have been given by others;

· Those whom you don't know but would like to meet—you have to make your own way with them.

You will, after a while, develop certain paragraphs that you can use over again as you write different kinds of letters, but at least in the beginning, each letter should be tailor-made for the recipient. There are two main types of letters:

1. The direct contact letter. A mutual acquaintance has suggested that you get in touch. You mention something about the acquaintance, tell specifically what it is that you're looking for—this is important; if you arrange a meeting this person is going to spend at least forty-five minutes talking with you, so don't waste time—and then say that you will call. And then call and set up a meeting.

Sample "Direct Contact" Letter

WILLIAM B. NEWHALL
100 Cedar Tree Rd.
Weston, CT. 06883

Mr. Pierre LeClerque
President
Tricolor Capital Corporation
405 Lexington Avenue
New York, NY 10174

Dear Mr. LeClerque:

Mr. John Lyons, Managing Partner of Smith Brothers, has suggested that I contact you. We had been talking about my interest in meeting U.S.-based heads of French businesses and he mentioned the role your division plays in Tricolor's expansion plans.

By way of brief background, I have both domestic U.S. and overseas experience in the development and direction of industrial companies—with expertise in start-ups, buy-outs, financial planning, management studies, marketing, and process production. Specifically, from 1982 until recently, I served as managing director of a specialty chemical subsidiary based near Paris. Since return to the United States, I have been engaged in negotiating the purchase of a competitor to end a price war.

Mr. Lyons feels that since I have lived and worked in France and am familiar with Tricolor, there may be areas of mutual interest between your holding company and myself. Your recent acquisition activities further prompt my interest.

Although I do not know your specific plans, I would welcome the opportunity to meet with you. I will telephone your office soon for an appointment.

Sincerely,

---

2. *The direct interest letter.* In this situation, there is no go-between; you are writing without benefit of personal introductions. Obviously, the kind of vague letter that our survey respondents complained of will not do. Tie your letter into something: "I noticed in your last annual report that you are expanding your mining operations. My own background in metallurgical engineering and plant supervision might possibly dovetail with . . ."

Whatever kind of letter you write, and you will probably be writing many during your job campaign, be sure you make it clear that you understand what the corporation or institution does. Also be clear about what contributions you can make. It may be that your letter recipient knows of something suitable at another company. But unless your letter impresses, it's going to end up in a wastebasket rather than a to-be-looked-at-in-the-future stack.

Sometimes a newspaper or journal advertisement can give a job seeker a lead for a possible direct interest letter.

Henry Crichton, for example, had spent his career on Wall Street as an account executive. Reorganized out of his job in a major marketing shift by his firm, Henry wanted out of selling stocks to investors—he was bored.

More administrative and analytical than most Wall Street account executives, Henry sensed the potential of the sparsely populated

Sample "Direct Interest" Letter

WILLIAM B. NEWHALL
100 Cedar Tree Rd.
Weston, CT. 06883

Mr. M. G. Price
President
Hall Corporation
30 Rockefeller Plaza
New York, NY 10112

Dear Mr. Price:

I have followed your company with considerable interest for some time, being particularly impressed by the investment community's regard for your performance. It is intriguing to read how your earnings are expected to increase further as you continue to benefit from a flow of new products and a growing international presence. These developments prompt my letter.

By way of brief introduction, I am an executive with biomedical-product experience in domestic and overseas markets. This experience includes the strategic introduction of fluid-clarification equipment into highly competitive environments where an understanding of various national needs and purchasing habits makes a clear difference.

While I have no idea what your staffing plans might be at this time, I would welcome the opportunity to meet with you. I will telephone your office soon for an appointment.

Sincerely,

field of proxy solicitation firms—long before the tumult of almost daily corporate raids. So small was the field in Henry's city that his target list ran to only three firms. By coincidence, one advertised early in his campaign for a lawyer to be part of the firm's service capability.

In view of Henry's deficiency—he was not an attorney—we urged him to discover the name of the firm's president and write a letter of "direct interest," and thereby finesse the ad's requirement. The president seemed impressed by the interest Henry expressed in his letter—at least enough to grant an interview when Henry called to follow up.

During that meeting Henry clinched the deal by his response to one of the president's questions: "Do you think you can make cold calls?" he asked.

"Well, how do you think I got here?" was Henry's inarguable answer.

There is one other kind of letter that we hope you will write soon: that is the letter in which you accept a job offer. We mention it in passing because very few new employees—except those at the very tip of the pyramid—sign contracts these days.

Your letter of acceptance can have legal validity, and in it you will summarize your responsibilities and benefits, as well as monetary compensation, as you understand them. It is a good idea to include your interpretation of your work-related duties, and a rundown of the hierarchy to which you think you're responsible. Know who your boss is—and have it in writing. In these days of abrupt firings, you could find yourself assigned to the one person in the company whom you would rather quit than work for—so try to protect yourself.

Sample of Letter "Accepting an Offer"

WILLIAM B. NEWHALL
100 Cedar Tree Rd.
Weston, CT. 06883

Mr. Charles A. Brinkley
Senior Vice-President
Mega Corps.
200 Park Avenue
New York, NY 10017

CONFIDENTIAL

Dear Charles:

As I indicated over the phone, I am extremely pleased to have this opportunity to formally accept your offer to join Mega Corps. as Vice-President, Director of Finance for International, reporting to you. The process of getting to know the company, your goals, and the people involved has been extraordinary, and I look forward to the happiest of associations.

In reflecting on our discussions, I thought you might appreciate a summary of my understandings about objectives, responsibilities, authority, and compensation. In brief, they are:

You have a personal commitment to management-by-objectives in order to maximize the potential impact of the finance and control function on Mega's performance;

The responsibilities of my position will be those outlined in the position description you provided me and which have been agreed to among yourself, Dale Jones, and Gerald Barnes;

As the Vice-President, Director of Finance for International, I will have your full support to establish priorities, direct related activities, and secure appropriate relationships with other corporate operations. Additionally, I will have the same support to create an internal finance organization;

It is your intent to have the chief financial person for each area begin a formal reporting relationship to me by June, 1988.

Specifically with regard to compensation, my understanding is that my package will include:

A starting salary of $150,000 with a to-start bonus of $15,000;

Participation in the Management Incentive Program for the fiscal year on a pro-rata basis;

Award of options to purchase common shares, the nomination for such an award to occur during the first six months of employment.

In our conversation of November 19, you established the company's commitment to a reward system which implies an atmosphere of mutual trust and allows for competitive compensation increases consistent with performance.

As a last point, it is my understanding that in the unlikely event a change of corporate strategy dictates a retrenchment in the company's plans for the International division that would impact negatively on my function, the company would either transfer me to another, suitable assignment or provide me with reasonable support in securing another position outside the organization.

In conclusion, Charles, I am most excited about Mega Corps. and this opportunity to work for you in the growth of the company's international operations. My family and I look forward to a rewarding relationship with everyone.

Sincerely,

Communicate! Your Skills on the Job-Campaign Trail

Now that your résumés are printed and you've psyched yourself into a positive, eager frame of mind, where are you going to start? You've looked in the newspaper and responded to ads, but they didn't look very promising; and indeed, no one has called you back.

You have talked to a few recruiters, but you don't match any current assignment they are handling, but they will call you if they hear of something suitable. You don't have a good feeling about that either.

The fact is, what you see listed in the paper—although you should answer any suitable ads—and hear from recruiters is only the tip of the job-opportunity iceberg; the very tip, probably not more than 20 percent. That means there remains 80 percent that seems to be invisible: that is more or less what it is, and it is called the "hidden market." It is not really "hidden"—it is that we don't know how to recognize what's right in front of us.

These "hidden market" jobs are those that are going to be filled by word of mouth because it is much more comfortable for the employer to find someone who comes recommended by someone he knows, likes, and trusts.

Or these are jobs that haven't opened up yet. Charles is going to retire at the end of the year, and everybody knows it and is keeping an eye out for a good replacement, but no one wants to advertise the job in the newspaper. Or a company has just acquired a small firm to strengthen a unit inside the organization and someone may be needed to "administer" the costing of a new product these combined companies will offer to the marketplace.

There are positions that have never existed before, until you have lunch with the vice-president because he's your college roommate's ex-husband and he realizes that your public relations expertise is just what he needs to get the Chicago office going.

This is the job that you hear about because you fall into conversation with a businessman on a flight from Los Angeles to New York, and it turns out that the company he works for is opening a San Francisco office. It has no staff at all as yet; "give their California-based executive vice-president a call and here's his phone number; and be sure to tell him that I told you to call."

Networking

To tap into the hidden market you will need to make use of that resource that we have been discussing throughout this book: your network. Actually, your network comes in two shapes. The better-known one is that group of friends, relatives, and colleagues who are

NETWORKING·RESOURCES·OPPORTUNITY

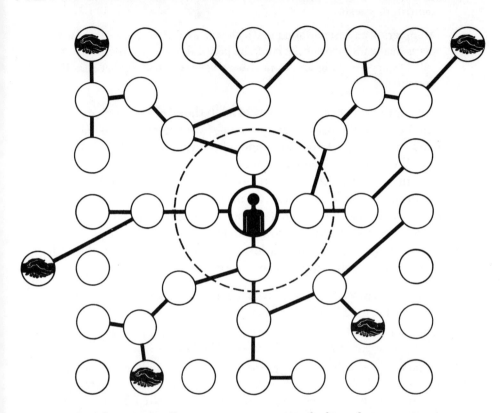

Networking: Your efforts can activate an interlocking chain reaction composed of people you know and people they know. Our experience suggests that among them may be the contact that you need to successfully complete your search.

willing to help you by giving advice and counsel, passing your name along to anyone who might be able to help, or telling you to contact someone directly.

This primary network usually refers mostly to your colleagues in a business milieu, but it could include practically anyone in your address book:

· Coworkers and previous employers, suppliers from any job.

· All friends, relatives, in-laws, friends of friends.

- "The Old School Tie": school chums, former professors.

- Your professional support staff—accountant, lawyer, banker, broker, dentist, physician.

- Members of any organization in which you are active or at least show up occasionally for meetings: it could be political, religious, social, theatrical, literary—as long as the members have an idea of what it is that you do.

Some of these people may know of a job themselves—and give you a name to call. But most will give you a network referral—the name of someone who might know someone who might know of something. It's like the proverbial snowball effect.

This then, is the second type of network: it's defined as "the strength of the weak tie." You call all these people, no matter how unlikely. Someone has estimated that to receive one job offer you have to have ten interviews, so get started.

You're going to be making a lot of phone calls, so think through your telephone technique before you begin.

1. It's polite to precede your call with a note. Introduce yourself, tell why you're going to call and when, and then do it.

2. Don't waste the listener's time. Know exactly what you want—to set up an appointment; some information—and be brief.

3. Imagine the schedule of the person whom you're calling. It's not very thoughtful to call first thing Monday morning, when he or she is trying to get started on the week. Tuesdays are better, and on Thursdays and Fridays you're likely to find a more cheerful group of executives.

4. Be prepared to talk to a secretary or assistant. Be pleasant and open with this person, who might very well hold the key to your being able to set up a meeting. If you can't get through to your main objective, be cheerfully persistent. As long as you are, the assistant will eventually relent. We don't think that executives are offended by persistence, just by an arrogant me-first attitude. So persevere, and keep your sense of humor.

5. If you're uncomfortable using the phone, write down what you want to say. No one will ever know. Of course, you can't script the other person's remarks, so you'll have to wing it a little. We predict that by the time your job search has reached a successful conclusion, the telephone will seem like an extension of yourself.

Think of the telephone as a useful tool. Some executives today would rather deal with a quick phone call than have to open, read, and answer a letter on any subject, especially concerning someone whom they don't know well or at all.

Swain & Swain is in partnership with other outplacement firms worldwide called Outplacement International. At a recent meeting we asked them how they felt contact was best made in the job search process in general and in networking in particular: by phone or letter? Although we did receive responses supporting the letter-first method of initial introduction, others thought that more effective than a contact letter is a personal phone call from a "go-between" contact to open the door.

As you establish your network you can think of yourself as being in command of a radar scope: it is the light band extending out from the center point—in your case, looking for information, and you frequently do not know what will appear on the screen.

According to our networking survey, some executives are beginning to feel that this actually is becoming burdensome: they're inundated with requests for their time, for their advice, and for their contacts. Some networkers, they feel, seem to think that they have the right to take up a great deal of time without offering anything in return.

A warning: Do be thoughtful. State your business, get your information, and leave. Also, once you get started, you are part of the network too. It is your responsibility to furnish as well as receive aid and information.

JOB-SEARCH NETWORKING: IS IT WORKING?

This survey taken in 1983 by Swain & Swain reveals a sharp split in attitudes toward job-search networking—with the predominant side holding that the process is misused and overworked and the smaller side holding that networking is a fine idea and should be utilized more fully.

The survey was sent to 500 executives, managers, and professionals across the country. Many of the respondents were critical of networking—a process in which they are called upon to contribute time and suggestions to job seekers. One expressed it this way: "Unfortunately, with high unemployment, networking has been overused and sometimes abused. Some know how to network, while others have only read or heard just enough to misuse the process."

What Motivates Executives to Participate in Networking?

For the less frequently networked executives, the motive seems to be altruism—believing that the job seeker will benefit from their experience and suggestions. The more frequently networked executives seem less confident about the benefits of networking, but are motivated to see a networking job seeker if they are attracted to the individual's background or are impressed by how much the individual knows about them (through well-informed colleagues, generally, as opposed to less well-informed social friends). But dark clouds appear to be gathering over job-search networking as the more frequently involved executives show signs of weariness from demands on their time.

Network Meetings—When, Where, and for How Long?

Eighty-five percent of the respondents prefer to meet networkers during office hours. Only 10% like breakfast meetings, and only 5% favor meeting for lunch (possibly because of uncertainty over who should pay the bill). This preference for office hours seems to reflect a concurrent desire to limit these meetings to 30 minutes. Very few respondents welcome the prospect of long meetings.

What Causes Executives to Avoid the Networking Job Services?

Approached more frequently, heavily involved executives will avoid the job seeker if they: are just too busy to see a networker; think too little benefit could result; are put off by the networker's approach. Not as taxed (or as weary yet of the process), the less frequently involved executives tend not to meet with the job seeker only if they are too busy.

What Do Job Seekers Get from Networking?

Ideally, information and introductions, leading to the discovery of job opportunities. In practice, the survey indicates that results seem to be a function of how experienced the participants are with networking. The frequently involved executives more often provide names of other people to contact. The less frequently involved executives (possibly puzzled by the vague agenda of many job-seeking networkers) tend to give less information about emerging possibilities—maybe not understanding how this could be helpful.

How Can Job Seekers Improve Networking Results?
As one executive responded, "The most effective networking seems to result when the job campaign is clearly and specifically focused. Otherwise, effort spent in developing the network will be wheel-spinning." This belief about the need to be focused was expressed by 95% of the frequently networked executives, while 70% of the less frequently involved respondents held that job seekers should provide clearer statements of how the networked executive could be helpful. The majority of respondents at both levels of networking involvement thought that job seekers could be more careful about the use of time spent together in network meetings. As one respondent added, "Over the years, I have found properly managed networking to be useful. The key is to establish a network made up of strong links, using several contacts to whom the job seeker is known to establish the base, and branching out in an orderly and personalized way. There is no substitute for the leveraged potential of personal contacts for at least a door-opening introduction."

The Open Market

Although networking will be your most important source of employment information, we do not mean for you to neglect the more obvious job listings: the open market.

1. *Advertisements.* These represent, by and large, sincere efforts on the part of employers to find qualified candidates for positions. If you're a specialist in some field, like aerospace, you might see something attractive in a technical journal.

2. *Contingency search firms.* If you know exactly what sort of job you're looking for, register with those that specialize in your field.

3. *Retainer search firms.* These companies are retained by corporations to fill specific jobs as they become available; there is often a close relationship between the search firm and the corporation, and over a period of time there develops a clear understanding of what sort of employee the company likes. The corporation's demands are often quite specific—they want a particular cluster of traits and skills to fill a particular job.

James H. Kennedy, publisher of *Consultants News* and other publications relating to the executive search field, who probably knows more about the ways of these firms than anyone else, thinks that the term "matchmaker" is much more appropriate than "headhunter."

It is up to the executive search firm to find that *exact* fit. If you happen to send them a résumé and you "match," you may be given a call and an interview set up. But, as Paul Slater points out, the odds are very long indeed against your backgrounds matching exactly the narrow specifications prescribed by the corporate client. You must have the *exact* qualifications. Timing is key.

On the other hand, continues Slater, "it doesn't hurt to be in touch with executive search firms; you might get lucky." In order for the executive search firm to consider your résumé carefully, however, your cover letter plus résumé should, according to Slater, be clear about "what you are looking for; how you feel about a possible geographical relocation; and what your current compensation is or has been."

The general advice from those dealing with executive search firms seems to be that although you can't depend on their finding a matchup between you and one of their current search assignments, it would be foolhardy for you to overlook search firms entirely. Send along your résumé with a cover letter containing the three points mentioned above by Paul Slater.

Answering An Ad

WILLIAM B. NEWHALL
100 Cedar Tree Rd.
Weston, CT. 06883

February 12, 1987

Mr. James Grimes
President and General Partner
Ventures Associates
425 Park Avenue
New York, NY 10017

Dear Mr. Grimes:

This is in response to your search for a General Manager to take XYZ Technologies' products to the consumer and commercial markets. This is a type of challenge with which I have considerable experience, which prompts me to be a candidate for the position. In addition, I am familiar with your parent company and have considerable respect for its personnel, extraordinary growth, and success.

With regard to your requirements, I possess the following background:

Take the Product to Consumer and Commercial Markets
My background includes experience in managing the marketing and sales of engineered products to both these markets through direct marketing, manufacturer's reps, private labeling, two-step distribution, direct response, and catalogue houses. The majority of this activity has been introducing newly developed products to highly competitive markets, achieving targeted results.

Be Responsible for Financial Management
As a key management member of the U.S. subsidiary of a foreign company, I have exercised responsibility for setting financial goals, managing performance against plan,

controlling net contribution, and (more recently) net operating income.

Work with Contract Manufacturers

Early in my career, I worked closely with manufacturing personnel to achieve new-product development and cost-reduction programs. Beginning in 1980, I sought and located a number of private-label manufacturers, assisted them in developing their marketing/merchandising plan, and monitored their delivery of specified products to various markets and customers. This responsibility heavily involved me in the negotiation of price, terms, conditions, and inventory levels.

Strong Background in Marketing Consumer Products

My strength is that of a general manager with special ability to introduce new products to diverse markets, expand market share, build a sales and marketing organization, and establish strong customer relationships at all levels. Related areas of expertise include forecasting, pricing, field sales management, advertising, and sales promotion.

My specific consumer-product experience spans: decorative molding for household use, garden equipment, water-insulation products, and packaging materials (for beverages, food products, and specialty additives).

Be Entrepreneurial, Highly Motivated, and Bright

I have continually sought out new product "frontiers" and enjoyed and been successful in introducing new products to diverse markets.

In 1979 I joined the newly incorporated U.S. subsidiary of an entrepreneurial-minded European company, and was a key factor in building a manufacturing and marketing company with total U.S. distribution to the consumer and commercial markets from scratch.

Most recently, as President of the ABC Products Company, I have started up a product line and launched it into the consumer and commercial market. My responsibilities have been carried out with high personal motivation—and it is this characteristic which I impart easily to my colleagues and subordinates. With regard to brightness, I welcome and enjoy the intellectual challenges of business and fast-changing marketplaces.

Some Additional Thoughts—
I believe that your market is in the beginning of a remarkable growth stage which will be driven by increased governmental attention and increased public awareness.

Even though there are a number of similar products now on the market, it is my opinion that a clear market and technology leader has not yet emerged which really understands the consumer and total commercial market opportunities in the United States and internationally.

Well financed, with proprietary technology, and market-driven, XYZ could be the company to capture this leadership position, especially when coupled with an entrepreneurial General Manager with knowledge and experience in introducing new products into the consumer and commercial markets.

I look forward to meeting with Ventures Associates to further discuss this exciting and challenging opportunity.

Sincerely,

The Interview

The point of all these preparations, of course, is to arrange an interview, an event for which you will want to be at your best.

The interview is obviously a great deal more than a simple conversation between friends in which you try to find out if a job interests you and they try to discover if you're the sort of person whose background and personality qualify you to be one of them.

A few pointers:

1.   *Be meticulous about your appearance.*   You will naturally be looking your best in a suitable businesslike way. No run-over heels, no clanging jewelry, clothes spotless and pressed.

2.   *Be on time.*   Leave lots of time if you live in an area where transportation is erratic and trains are often stalled. There are almost no excuses possible if you're late for a job interview—and why start with such a disadvantage?

3.   *Be positive.*   Be enthusiastic without burbling. And never, never bad-mouth your previous employer. One of the hard questions you will almost certainly be asked is "Why are you looking?" A brief, truthful, nondefensive response is the best avenue for you to take: "My division was eliminated." There is never any reason to go into personality conflicts.

4.   *The interview process is a two-way affair.*   See the interviewer as a real person with opinions, feelings, and a mission to accomplish; you can be a nurturer in this instance.

5.   *Be prepared.*   Learn all you possibly can about the company, its products, its philosophy, its personnel. And you will have some idea where you might fit into the organization.

6.   *Allow the interviewer to control the flow of the interview.*   Pay close attention to the questions and be sure you understand them.
   In addition, Swain & Swain clients are coached:

7. *Allow yourself to be interrupted.* Remember that the typical person's attention span while you are answering a question is no more than two minutes. Don't babble.

8.   *Be careful of what and how much you say.*   All too many good candidates for top jobs have lost out to lesser competition because they talked too much.
   Be alert to seemingly general questions like, "Tell me a little about yourself." Keep your answer focused on your positioning statement: "Well, I see myself as a general manager with extensive experience in . . ."

No matter how sympathetic the interviewer appears, keep personal information for a later time. Do not meander through your life history.

9.   *Keep the main point of the interview in mind.*   You are there to tell the company why it would be a good investment for them to hire you as a resource. They want an employee who will fit in with their company culture and who will make them money. It is your task to indicate that you are that person. This involves extrapolating from your past work experience all those successes that apply; as well as demonstrating a real understanding of the potential difficulties in the job being discussed. You want them to see you as a useful resource in which they would be wise to invest.

10.   *On the subject of salary.*   If the corporation or institution is interested in you, they will want to know what their investment will have to be. Remember the old adage that "the first person who mentions money loses."

What might the interviewer be thinking? We asked Eleanor H. Raynolds, a partner in the executive search firm of Ward Howell International, what she looked for during an initial interview—what triggered a positive first impression. Ellie's list:

· Suitable dress and a generally neat appearance.

· Firm handshake.

· Pleasant speaking voice and a good vocabulary.

· Good energy level.

· A little humor.

· An enthusiastic, upbeat manner.

· Attentive expression during the interview and good listening ability.

· A clear, easily understood résumé.

· Apparent ability to accept a risk.

· The ability to articulate past accomplishments in a clear and concise manner.

As you prepare yourself for an interview, remember that the company has an agenda, too. They might be as anxious to fill a position as you are to find one.

At a Swain & Swain workshop dedicated to the "stress of the interview," one of our clients, Charles Dorsey, recounted a telling story from his corporate past.

It seemed that Charles had requested of his company president that a new position be created in his organization to handle a vexing market-support issue.

The president agreed and Charles began his search. A suitable candidate was found, wooed, and an offer was made. The candidate asked for several weeks to consider the offer.

All told, eight weeks had elapsed from the time Charles made the original request and he was dismayed to hear that after all this time his candidate was turning the offer down in order to remain with his present company. With this setback, Charles felt acute pressure when the president asked about the search at the next staff meeting. Charles told of the rapidly accelerating nervousness he felt in resuming his search and beginning to interview new candidates. He knew that he had to find the right person, and be quick about it, too.

If we had a gift to give you during the search process—other than the perfect new job—it would be patient perseverance. It pays off, but we know that it's difficult to go through the seemingly endless tasks of letter writing and calling and interviewing without a brass ring in clear view.

Accept our experience and that of others that the hard work will pay off handsomely if your campaign is intelligently conceived and pursued honestly. Our experience has borne this out—there are exciting new opportunities developing constantly.

AN OVERVIEW

THE SWAIN & SWAIN INDIVIDUAL PROGRAM

PART ONE

First Meeting

Introduction
- introduction to situation
- what happened and why are you here?
- thoughts on what to do next
- develop background information

Background
- what have you done during your career?
- analysis of skills and abilities
- self-assessments

Second Meeting

History
- discuss results of self-assessment
- review of work history
- develop list of related accomplishments

Positioning
- where do you see yourself going?
- what types of roles will you play?
- which organizations are you best suited for?

Third Meeting

Potential Market
- examine potential marketplace:
  companies, industries, organizations

The Résumé
- develop a résumé: objective and/or
  background summary, career history,
  education, other interests

Fourth — Seventh Meetings

Plan of Action
- develop a network
- who to contact and what to say
- list target companies and key individuals
- develop a schedule for most effective
  use of time

Implementation
- role-play questions and answers
- write letters for contacts, recruiters, direct
  interests, ads
- fine-tune
- review

PART TWO

The Campaign
- follow up on letters, leads
- make phone calls
- secure interviews and informational
  meetings
- continue to build and fine-tune
  interview skills

PART THREE

The Finish
- get offers
- negotiate terms: base, bonus, benefits, perks
- evaluate choices and make decision
- accept offer

Outline of campaign strategy that we use at Swain & Swain

Chapter VIII
Gender Is More Than a Six-Letter Word

Gender (n.)—either masculine or feminine. The masculine is divided into temperate and intemperate, and feminine into frigid and torrid.—[anon.]

T HE behavioral differences of men and women are long and well noted—and are the kinds of differences that depend largely on the demands of the society in which the sexes find themselves. The subject can be approached from many points of view: nature versus nurture; the women's movement; Freudian psychology; child-rearing practices in the industrialized nations; the dearth of women researchers in physics; etc., etc., etc.

Let us take for granted that these factors have a bearing on all the present-day dynamics of human behavior—and the resulting endless possibilities of interrelationships and self-analysis. It is true that we are taking enormous chunks of Western psychology, sociology, and history as givens, but in order to be helpful to you, the reader, we need to focus on matters specific to your concerns. In the course of looking for a job you will be meeting, and being interviewed by, both men and women. No doubt your day-to-day life includes interaction with both, but you should note that massive reorganizations and the resulting transformation of the managerial pyramid are not the only revolutionary changes going on in corporate America today.

The Two-Gender Work Force

It's important for every job seeker—especially the men—to understand that although some segments of our business and political establishment are reluctant to accept the reality as presented by available statistics—women have arrived in the marketplace in force and they are there to stay.

There is a riddle from the early days of the feminist movement that goes like this: A little boy is playing on the swings in a park, supervised by his father. He swings too high, falls, and injures himself badly. He is rushed to the hospital, and surgery is indicated.

Enter the surgeon, who says: "I cannot possibly operate on this child. He is my son."

What's going on here? We've already met the feckless father, in the park where the accident occurred. Could there be two fathers?

Perhaps the answer is obvious to us today, but it wasn't twenty years ago: the surgeon is the boy's *mother.*

Whether you're male or female, you're going to encounter women at all levels of the managerial hierarchy as you job-hunt. Women may interview you and women may decide whether or not to hire you and a woman may be your boss.

It was not long ago that such a situation would have been unimaginable. Those are the days of "Ozzie and Harriet" and "Father Knows Best," with the TV families in which Dad went off to a vaguely defined place of employment and Mom tended the hearth and was an all-round support system. But today less than a *third* of America's families fit into the category of "traditional" families.

There are today 49 million women in the work force, and by 1990 more than half of that work force will be female. As of this writing, in 1987, 70 percent of all women between the ages of twenty-five and fifty-four have jobs, and by 1995, it is expected that 81 percent of women aged twenty-five to thirty-four will be at the workplace. That leaves very few at home to take care of the children. And who is taking care of the children? Other business people, in part. The child care industry is flourishing and nannies are in demand.

Change within America's institutions generally happens because of the pressures of necessity. When women became stridently vocal, and got enough power brokers to see things their way, they got the vote. We are today on the brink of far-reaching if reluctantly implemented change within our corporations. Corporate America is going to need women during the next decade—and it will need them on a managerial level.

Is Behavior Predictable?

Will women's increasing presence lead to the feminization of the workplace? Perhaps in part. But America's businesses and institutions would have to adapt a great deal before the prevailing macho image is altered in any real way.

We know that anything we say about male or female personality traits and resulting behavior must be understood to be guideposts only. There are lots of four-year-old girls who show little interest in dolls and like nothing better than to spend an afternoon with their toy roofing set. And there are young women today who are catching rivets on construction sites and driving buses with the best of the men. There are males in our society who are wonderfully nurturing; who are poetic and creative; who are finding careers in areas formerly reserved for women—such as nursing. Let us therefore accept as fact that no one person even comes close to incorporating all the traits of any textbook stereotype, and for any stereotype whom you might encounter in a work situation there exists its unpredictable counterpart.

But, having said all that, we do believe that there are generalizations that are at least partly true and that can give you clues to possible behavior patterns that you might meet as you thread your way through the maze of interviews that constitutes a job search, or contemplate accepting a particular job offer.

Although men in reality display different sorts of managerial styles, the ideal model is that of the tough strategist: he is rational, assertive, highly competitive, has a sense of humor, but can be emotionally detached.

Men have been running the managerial show for so long that this style is the prototype by which all managers—men and women—are judged. And, indeed, if approved management styles filter down from the executive suite, it is certainly a male-based model. Although women have made great inroads into the ranks of middle management—in fact, 9.2 percent of all working women are executives—they make up only about 1 percent of the top executive class.

What this means for the woman middle manager is a serious lack of female role models and mentors. Men have always had mentors and role models and have used them to modify or even create their own managerial behavior.

And although the corporate world can be a great socializer—just think of the rigid corporate cultures that develop in which the employees look alike and think alike, as a team, or go elsewhere— women are not usually easily integrated into the male ethos of aggressive confidence (which may be real or feigned), crafty deal-making, and sports-based camaraderie. To the woman manager, it appears that even the most unlikely males seem to have the statistics of the local major-league ball team on the tips of their tongues. Sometime the woman's attempt to match him produces outrageous remarks like: "The batter scored a touchdown and won the game," or "He got the ball on the kick-off and took it to the 100-yard line."

As outsiders, women have often been left to establish their own managerial style—which is, naturally enough, a function of the way in which they normally deal with the outside world.

What might you expect if you are a man or woman and are offered a job working for a woman? Or what sort of person should you be prepared for if you are to be interviewed by a middle- or top-level female manager?

"Traditional women's values," says Dr. Natalia Zunino, a New York City psychotherapist, "are based on affiliation. They prefer to solve problems through cooperation, using their close relationships with other people. Men's behavior, on the other hand, is still governed by the dual traits of competitiveness and assertiveness."

Yet, oddly enough, we encounter men in our outplacement work that are seriously put off by the prospect of being interviewed by a woman. They fail to imagine any role for the woman interviewer other than the "strict and critical elementary school teacher"—and an "old maid, at that."

Until recently, if women wanted promotions and responsibility, it was implicit in their unwritten agreement with the corporation or institution that had hired them that they would model their behavior as much as possible after that of the male managers: "competitiveness" and "assertiveness," in Dr. Zunino's terms.

As always, there are exceptions: Helen Gurley Brown, the editor who found a whole new and faithful market for Hearst's *Cosmopolitan* magazine, has always had her own very feminine managerial style. She was never influenced in the least by Hearst's rather serious corporate culture—but by dint of charm, persistence, and considerable marketing talent, she has shepherded *Cosmo* into the eighties on her own editorial terms. But Helen Gurley Brown started at the top in the Hearst organization—she was hired as editor in chief—which makes a difference.

What happened to those women who wanted a managerial career but couldn't start near the top in an organization?

They did what was expected of them and became tough managers, devoted to their jobs. Indeed, some became so devoted that they never developed full lives for themselves outside the office. Like so many other managers, these experienced women are now being caught up in the massive reorganization that is displacing so many workers—and some are ending up in our offices.

The typical female executive who comes to Swain & Swain for outplacement is about forty-four-years old and has worked her way up to a "reasonable" rung of the corporate ladder. Not too many are earning megabucks, mostly because they started out at the low-going rate of twenty years ago and have remained loyal to just a few employers—on an average they have been with their most recent employers for ten years—so have not job-hopped their way to higher salaries.

What we have found telling is that nearly 70 percent of this group have never married—an extremely high percentage when compared with American women in general and young female managers in particular. We can only assume that the struggle to reach the middle levels of management took so much time and energy that this earlier work generation of women didn't have the time to set up complicated households of their own.

Although we do hate to generalize, they *have* often modeled their managerial behavior on detached, aggressive, coldly efficient male models and do their jobs superseriously. They may be intimidating and hard to reach. As a candidate for a job, your most businesslike demeanor is suitable in this sort of interview situation.

If you're a woman and you've been offered a job in this type of manager's department, be warned that women so dedicated are often more demanding of other women than they are of their male staff.

They came up the hard way, set high standards for themselves, and see no reason why you shouldn't also. Their attitude can be, "I'm in the boat, pull up the ladder."

If you think you can't bear such a rough approach, you should job-hunt elsewhere, but crusty personalities sometimes mellow with time—the time you would spend in her department learning things that could be invaluable. If you're tough enough, you perhaps could put up with a little unpleasantness for the sake of excellent training and experience.

But chances are that you will encounter a younger woman manager—one who has been promoted to her present position recently.

Her leadership style is more likely to resemble that described earlier by Dr. Zunino—with its reliance on intuition rather than analytical problem-solving, cooperation rather than competition, and humanistic concern for the long-term ambience of the organization rather than on the short-term quick fix. Men will often try to win outright—and they want their opponent to lose. But women—and this is a positive introduction to management style—often try to establish a win-win situation, in which both parties are satisfied with the result.

But some women managers of this newer generation have had problems in their corporate environment—and their problems could become yours.

Over the years we have noticed that we were getting a disproportionate number of women in outplacement. They all told us, naturally, why in their opinion they had been displaced. But the reasons they gave us were not the reasons we heard from the sponsoring companies: overwhelmingly, their previous employers felt that these women were just not good managers.

To make the situation even more painful, women often are much more devastated than men when they are asked to leave a job. It is in situations like this that a man's level-headed rationalism is useful. But many women have made considerable sacrifices in order to put in the time needed at their corporations and are shocked and incredulous when they're let go.

Women are often not as tuned-in as men to the realities of corporate politics; a woman may rely on how she "feels" about a situation and not realize that change is imminent and that her job is in jeopardy. Women are often less ruthless than men, and may view themselves and their staff as individuals, although a more sensible approach would be to look at the bottom line—are she and her staff producing revenue for the company?

Women seem to react to their immediate environment and respond positively to feedback. They like to problem-solve with others; consensus suits them. Many need more praise to reassure them of their own self-worth and they want their employer to value them. (A man, on the other hand, often will be satisfied with an excellent rating of his job performance alone.)

If a woman has depended on her job for a positive self-image and feelings of worthiness, as so many of them have, the emotional attachment to a company can be extreme. It is not surprising that many feel abandoned when they are shown the door.

On the plus side, once women get over the shock of dismissal, they are often back on the job-hunting track more effectively than some men.

Susan Geisenheimer, Vice-President of Human Resources for the Time Inc. magazine group, has told us that "women are more open to psychological self-assessment, while it is often hard for men to acknowledge that they need help. Women, for example, are much more willing to open up and make good use of the outplacement process."

We agree. Because women are generally more in touch with their feelings, they are much more likely to be open with a counselor, see what's gone wrong, and do it better next time.

Is it true that women are *not* good managers, and should you, whether a man or woman, do everything in your power to stay out of their managerial way?

Once again, there are as many truths as there are women managers. But when women are not good managers, it is generally because they weren't trained in management skills on their way up.

Some women came to their present executive rank after having been very successful in a specialized job. This might be a woman's first job managing a large staff of men and women, for example. And a business school does not teach a manager how to be a boss—that's something you have to learn by doing.

The masculine experience in this country—while fostering desires to dominate and succeed—is also molded by various group experiences that women rarely have, or certainly not to the extent that men do: the military, and team sports from the time that they're old enough to understand the rules. But if you think women don't catch on quickly then you haven't seen enough youth league soccer.

Men are accustomed to training each other, and their socialization fits in neatly with the idea of the corporate team. They are used to hierarchical command, and know that if they follow the rules—which, being part of the ruling elite, they understand—they will be promoted.

But woman have had little such training, and because of that their methods of communication are a mélange of their socialization as women in this country added to their own interpretation of the corporate culture around them. Women do not always—indeed, do not often—enjoy the guidance of an experienced mentor, either male or female, nor do they have a large cohort of executive women like themselves for consultation and feedback. They can generally be found isolated on the front lines doing the best they can with only limited information as to how top management thinks and acts, and what they really want from their staff.

Many women have therefore developed a managerial style that is either natural to them, or that they think the predominantly male top management wants. And that style *is* different from that of men, which could mean trouble for you in an interview if you're male and not sensitive to the differences. You might also have difficulty with her if she is your boss and you haven't caught on to a new set of psychological ground rules.

In an interview, whether male or female, you will always do best to listen well and communicate on her terms if you want her to be interested in you and if you expect to get a clear idea of what the job is all about.

We've already mentioned that a woman's natural style is often based on consensus; it's affiliative and cooperative. This is appealing to many employees, but it may not be what you're used to if you were raised in the aggressive world of macho decision-making.

Remember that women tend to be more open and more direct than men, who may have been schooled in "play it close to the vest" tactics. The portrayal in literature of feminine wiles is really not often applicable to the female manager. Women are much more likely than men to say what's on their mind. So be prepared for it—and don't be frightened. The interviewer does not mean to be intimidating. She's just trying to get an accurate picture of you—quickly.

When the Boss Is a Woman—and You're Not

With some trepidation you, a man, have taken a job in a department managed by a woman.

If you're quite a young man, the adjustment might be easier than if you are in the middle years. You might, for example, have a wife with a serious career of her own and suffer no hangups about the women-in-the-workplace issue. In graduate school, you may have competed regularly for top grades with women who were smarter and more ambitious than you. You're pretty sure that you understand just how effective a woman manager can be.

But even men who fit into this category can't be too smug. Many have more deep-rooted assumptions about male superiority than they're willing to admit—it's still a strong theme in American culture.

If you're from an earlier generation, stereotypical thinking is no doubt even more ingrained. It may literally be impossible for you to work for a woman, especially one younger than you. You may see any woman on an executive level as out of her depth, nothing more than a silly little girl promoted beyond her abilities and competence—and have doubts about how she got where she is today.

If a stereotype is too ingrained, the scenario may end badly.

Joanne is president of a small public relations firm that she runs with her partner, Jim. Several years ago, they decided to bring in a seasoned executive to be the number-three person in the organization, to develop business by mounting an active sales effort. Ronald was their choice—an experienced executive in his fifties.

Ronald took to Jim right from the start and, ignoring Joanne, began letting staff and clients alike know that he and Jim were going to make a great team. Although Ronald's primary supervisor was to have been Joanne, he seemed reluctant from the very start to communicate with her about any of his activities. Joanne found herself rebuffed by every attempt to elicit information from him on his progress.

A final confrontation occurred about three months after Ronald joined the firm. Asked again for a monthly sales report, which had never materialized, Ronald blew his stack. Refusing to deal with Joanne, he stormed into Jim's office and said that he thoroughly resented having to answer to a woman and wouldn't stand for it. Jim said fine—he was free to carry on with his career, somewhere else.

It was later discovered that Ronald's previous boss had also been female and the word on him was that he had a "thing" about working for women.

Before you refuse a job that might be rewarding and suitable, contemplate Margaret Thatcher. Do you think that any man ever turned down a job working with her because she is a woman?

Your prospective boss might be more up-to-date in your field than you are and might even be able to teach you things. Raise your consciousness a little and see her as a person with talents—some that you may even lack—as well as foibles. Give her and yourself a chance. Think of yourself as a pioneer presaging the future, because women managers are gradually becoming commonplace.

It is true that in certain very manly fields—like heavy industry and the military—women will not be able to establish a toehold past the middle ranks until the current crop of management retires. They won't want women around and they're not going to hire them. And if they have to hire them, then they won't promote them. It will be up to the next generation to do that.

Anthropologists know that for an idea to become truly part of a culture, it must be based on reality of some sort—either culturally functional or spiritual. For example, although the top politicians in the USSR are men, women in that country enjoy much more managerial and professional equality than they do here. The Russian equality is rooted in opportunities offered two generations ago.

During World War II, women had to keep the country going while the men were at war. This also occurred in the United States, but the results were very different. Enough of our men returned from the battles in Europe and Asia to take their places in offices and factories, displacing the women who had stepped in to fill the gap under emergency conditions. We were very lucky not to have to fight on our own soil because the Russians lost more than 20 million citizens in the war with Germany; every person left was necessary for professional and industrial rebuilding.

It may take well into the next decade—during the predicted management shortage—for women to be needed desperately on the executive level. When that happens, gender distinctions will fade, women will receive fuller training, and stereotypes will disappear because management styles of men and women will be accepted—

and better understood. When that happens, a chapter such as this one will be obsolete.

You may very well have a woman manager who is respected for her functional expertise and is comfortable and effective in her job. She understands her subordinates and both teaches and allows them to learn on their own. She's a good manager, period. And she happens to be a woman.

But what if you're working for a woman (or, in fact, a man) who still carries the unnecessary and debilitating baggage that comes from "scarcity":

1. You ought to see her as a person who may have weak managerial skills, not as an incompetent female. Make sure that you do not emulate her management style to please her. If she manages absently, with no direction, you can manage yourself. You know how to organize your tasks. Be self-directed.

2. Even if you are de facto managing yourself, don't keep her in the dark. Find out early on which communications style she responds to—is it quantitative or qualitative? Does she appreciate a quick in-person briefing—or a long, detailed memo? Your boss needs feedback, but the manner in which you deliver it will be critical.

3. Know thyself. Are you frustrated and embarrassed by having to admit that you work for a woman? Think about what she does in detail. Is there something you can learn from the entire experience? Can you view this as a positive opportunity for you and your career?

4. In establishing your relationship, discover what she can do that you would like to learn. Ask to be trained.

5. Some women don't know how to "manage up"—they don't know how to establish good communications with *their* bosses. You may understand the corporate culture better than she just because you are a man. Help her. After all, she's your boss and she is certainly in a position to help *you* advance your career.

For Women: How to Succeed in Business Today

Until this emerging generation of managerial women, "She thinks like a man" was considered the highest accolade corporate management could bestow on any female employee.

And the women tried to live up to that image. They modeled their behavior after that of the most dynamic men—they were tough, they worked hard, they didn't let anyone put anything over on *them*, they wore three-piece suits and their lives centered around their jobs.

But today things truly are changing, because the employees insist on it; a corporation needs employees to function, and a lot of employees—about half—are women.

Women are simply no longer willing to become surrogate men in an office setting. More and more women have interests—and families— outside the office. Their life experiences have been very different from an earlier generation of managers, and they want to be able to develop their own management style; they're not in the least interested in growing up to be just like their tough, male bosses.

As we discussed earlier, corporations are being populated by both men and women with requests, and demands, for more flexible work situations. The campaign is bound to lead to more open, less dogmatic, corporate cultures, which would fit in well with a woman's natural managerial style—and ultimately benefit the progeny of today's male and female parents in the work force.

We've already touched on the pitfalls that our female readers might encounter if they have been trained as managers within the last few years. You might have received too little hands-on training in actually being a boss—you've been muddling through, sometimes with success and sometimes not. You've been relying on common sense and trial and error, but perhaps you might consider the following basics for good management. If you followed every one, you'd be Katharine Graham or Estée Lauder, but at the least know what your goals might be.

1. *The outer you no longer has to look as if you bought your clothes at Brooks Brothers.* There are many milieus in which suits are the usual business attire—law firms, corporate offices, anything in Washington, D.C.—but you can wear conservative dresses just as well. No longer does your own taste have to be totally submerged under a pinstriped three-piece suit, white shirt, and floppy foulard tie (an outfit that is held in contempt by most of the sophisticated trend-setters today) as long as what you choose is conservative.

And in your management style . . .

2. *Don't take yourself too seriously.* Sometimes women managers—especially those new to positions of responsibility—think that

all eyes are upon them and that if they laugh they will turn into a toad and also lose their job. Often a humorous touch helps out a difficult situation.

3. *Don't impose change for the sake of change.*   New managers can think that doing *anything* is better than doing nothing. At least then they seem to be in motion. But staff may be very resentful of pointless change, as it's a terrible waste of an employee's workday and probably won't help matters anyway. Bide your time when you're given a new managerial assignment and understand the structure of your department and the function of each team member before you decide that your way is the better way.

4. *Don't be afraid to say no.*   Some women fear that if they say no to any request from a subordinate—from a day off to a salary increase—they will be disliked. If you are, that's too bad, but it goes with the territory and not everyone is going to like you anyway.

5. *Listen to your employees.*   Find out what they like and don't like about their jobs. Some woman managers are too self-conscious to really hear what their employees are saying—they're too busy wondering if they're managing well and how their image is going over. The employee is much less interested in your image than how you can help him or her get a promotion.

6. *Be sensitive to other women.*   Sometimes it seems as if the women's movement never existed, and as if women are their own worst enemies.

To illustrate from our own experience: one of Swain & Swain's female counselors called a woman executive at a corporation that uses our outplacement service. The executive was out of the office, said her female secretary, but she would return the call. When the counselor hung up, she realized that the secretary—who did not know her—had called her by her first name throughout the conversation.

Bemused, the counselor experimented: she asked a male colleague—who was also unknown to the secretary—to call and see whether *he* would achieve immediate first-name status.

Of course he didn't. He was *Mr.* X from the first to the last. That secretary—and thousands like her—wouldn't dream of calling a man she didn't know by his first name.

What sort of message is that secretary transmitting to every woman who calls? One that is inappropriate for any executive's office staff and doubly so in an office where the boss is a woman. Remember, equality begins at home.

7. *Get used to your authority.* You will lose it if you don't use it. Your preferred style should be that of a group leader—you don't want to dominate or dictate. One of your strengths might very well be your willingness to stimulate group effort. But you should never delegate the final say in any important project—if you like, you can be first among equals, but you must be first.

8. *Never be vulgar.* In your effort to be "one of the boys," you may try an off-color remark or joke or use a four-letter word. The men may laugh, but they might also categorize you as "a loose cannon"— someone whom they can't take everywhere. Along the same lines, it's not a good idea to drink too much at lunch or an office function. Businesspeople in general drink a lot less than they used to, and you will find that most of your colleagues—including your boss—will not think it cute if after belting back a few with the boys you insist that the waiter dance with you.

9. *When a difficulty arises, don't automatically blame yourself.* "If something goes wrong in a work situation," says psychologist Dr. Natalia Zunino, "men often will look to externals for an explanation. Women are more likely to blame their own inadequacies."

You will without doubt make your share of mistakes, but you are not responsible for every computer failure or client who goes to a competitor. These are just results that you will do your best to fix. Be tough-minded and analyze what went wrong. Think of the best solution possible and forget the mea culpas.

Nobody wants to hear about how guilty you are and how everything happens to you.

10. *Do not be consciously seductive.* Some women do have a naturally seductive personality. They often were brought up in a society where flirting is expected of every girl from the time she is a toddler. It's very hard for women with this background to treat men in a completely businesslike way. But it is not appropriate to fix a man's tie, or lean close to smell his after-shave, or fix your eyes on his.

And other women are certainly going to be furious if they witness such a performance; somehow you're not sticking to the rules of how relationships between businesspeople—male or female—are conducted.

11. If you do have a romance with someone whom you met in a work situation, be prepared to have it end badly, especially if you're involved with your boss. An October 1986 issue of *Working Woman* magazine published the results of a survey of women on the subject of office romance. Forty percent of their sample *had* had office romances, most of which were with a coworker, or peer. An additional 19 percent were with a client or customer, and 39 percent were with a boss or other superior.

An affair with a boss made life at the office easier for 33 percent of the women, but for 23 percent it was a major problem. And although the percentages were not scientifically tabulated, the survey showed that if a woman had had several romances, she was much more likely to be fired than someone who had not had any office entanglement.

It seems clear that emotional involvement at the office can lead to unpleasant complications. Sometimes true love will conquer all—we know in inappropriate detail all about Mary Cunningham and William Agee—but what happens to you if the romance falls apart?

Are you really ready to pack up and look for another job to spare your erstwhile loved one the embarrassment of meeting you every morning at the coffee wagon? Just try to think of the consequences before you get involved, because the result may be that both of you cannot remain in one organization.

And finally . . .

12. It's never too late for you to try to find that valuable aid that most woman managers lack—a mentor. This person can be male or female, but will most likely be male just because there are so many more men in powerful positions.

Your relationship should be as reciprocal as possible—not all take on your part and give on his. You do, of course, want to learn as much as possible from this more experienced person, and it is understood that he will boost your career when he can. But do try to think of ways in which you can be helpful to him. He may, for example, want to talk about his work-related problems—everyone has them—and you could listen. Or, if you work in a different division, you could be a fount of useful information about the working of your part of the company. Look for opportunities to be useful.

But also hark back to rule number 11—it will be more helpful to your career if the relationship remains on a friendly but businesslike basis—one of mutual aid and appreciation.

The life of a woman manager can be full of uncertainty and difficulty in today's changing corporate world. It will be better for women in the next decade, and better still in the next century, but your lot *is* measurably easier than it was for your managerial predecessors.

Women in management have not yet reached the point at which their true personalities—ones that they're comfortable with—can be given free rein. Women are not wholly accepted in the corporate world and you may still encounter prejudice, male chauvinism, and jobs that you can't get because you're a woman.

And you may discover some failings in yourself that prevent you from being the successful manager that you had set out to be. But as times change, you will be given more opportunities to learn. Women managers will gain in strength as they gain in numbers.

The most useful advice we can think of for women who want to climb the ladder and gain leadership skills, is: look and listen—be aware of those around you, be compassionate, be willing to admit to shortcomings, and recognize that good interpersonal abilities separate the winners from the losers in any field.

Chapter IX
The Art of Negotiation

Negotiator (n.)—a fellow who says he's going to put his cards on the table, but wants an idea of your hand first.—[anon.]

THE art of negotiation is the art of compromise. We think of it as art because it takes knowledge and skill to properly conduct a transaction so that all parties feel satisfied. It is an art because it seems to happen too rarely that everyone goes home contented. And if you can orchestrate the win-win kind of negotiation that we at Swain & Swain advocate, it might even be high art.

"Negotiation" has a connotation of late nights with tough labor lawyers facing down the union leaders, but in its broader sense it is a concept that permeates every area of your life. You negotiate, or compromise, with your family, your boss, the person who's trying to charge too much to paint your car, and even fellow pedestrians that you share a sidewalk with in the morning rush hour. It's the *quid pro quo* of daily life: I'll give you something if I get something for me.

Negotiating may lead to a formal or an informal understanding. The young working couple agrees that each needs a night out from time to time just to have dinner with a friend—the other spouse will watch the kids. That's informal negotiation and subject to revision. Or a couple might be divorcing and the lawyers have finally brought the two principals to some kind of working agreement. This is formal negotiation and will lead to a binding agreement.

Effective negotiation is the basis for good management. It includes asking, explaining, convincing, and finally agreeing. Those men and

women who are most competent are articulate and level-headed—
they are assertive enough to make their points, but not so arrogant as
to lose the game. The very best negotiators need a sense of humor to
cool the situation down when tempers verge out of control and the
judgment of Solomon to understand both sides of a situation or
quarrel.

In this chapter, we're discussing good negotiating skills, mostly as
they're used in a work setting, but clearly these talents would be
useful to anyone trying to convince a fourteen-year-old daughter that
she's too young to stay out until 2:00 A.M., or a spouse that it's really
not in the family's best interest to have his or her unemployed brother
live with you.

At Swain & Swain, when we talk of negotiating we stress the aspect
of compromise—we don't think that negotiating to win everything is
a positive goal.

In a corporate or institutional setting, after all, we are not trying to
negotiate with the invader to get our homeland returned to us—we
are not dealing with world politics, but rather the microcosm of day-
to-day life. To add stress to our day is pointless, we just want an issue
resolved or a point made.

Dr. Tessa Albert Warschaw is a psychotherapist and corporate
consultant as well as the author of *Winning by Negotiation*. In her
book, Dr. Warschaw categorizes the four types of negotiators: "win-
lose," "lose-win," "lose-lose," and "win-win." Her description:

> Win-Lose Negotiators want to take home all the bacon. In order to do
> so, they must dominate the other person. . . . Their minds are totally
> fixed on victory. Lose-Win Negotiators gain what they want by losing
> . . . the last thing they want is to dominate. . . . Lose-Lose Negotiators
> can't stand the thought of the other person's winning, but they don't
> want to win, either. . . . Win-Win Negotiators want both parties to the
> negotiation to walk away winning, each with enough to show for his
> efforts for them still to be friends or partners. . . . Each party is willing
> to give up a certain amount in order to achieve this result.

We believe that win-win negotiating is so much the preferred
method that we suggest to our clients that they try to plan all their
work-related strategies—whether on the job or during the job
search—around this concept.

The win-win strategy can be helpful in the two most important
deal-making situations that you are likely to experience at this stage

in your life: when you negotiate your severance package and when you accept a job and agree on your salary, perks, and benefits.

Negotiating Your Way Out of the Corporation

Win-win negotiations as you prepare to leave your corporation are important because you may have an ongoing relationship with your about-to-be-ex employer for a very long time. You want them to think well of you, and you want to leave them with dignity.

Depending on your severance package, you will at least be in touch with the payroll and human resources departments for a time and you want everything to go smoothly from the administrative point of view—their administration. You're probably going to depend on them for a number of months for a paycheck, for insurance benefits, and resolution of stock option plans and savings incentive programs. When you are physically at the office, keep all your relationships reasonably friendly.

We're suggesting that you avoid making unnecessary enemies. As Mario Puzo's *Godfather* said, "Never give a gratuitous insult." If you manage a successful win-win negotiated departure, no ugly stories will make the rounds about your lack of cool and you can maintain those important business relationships.

Prospective employers or potential business partners are going to be calling your former colleagues for information about your skills and attitudes and you want those colleagues to be part of your friendly network. You will need the folks at your old company for friendship, industry information, and perhaps new opportunity ideas and leads.

There are many ways of being fired.

You may have known for a long time that your company was moving from its Chicago office to Nashville, Tennessee. Your husband has a job that he loves at the University of Chicago and your children are adolescents and would rather die than move. Your own job is not so unusual that you couldn't find something comparable, so you easily turn down the offer to join the company in Tennessee. You also have plenty of time to negotiate your severance package.

Or the handwriting on the wall has gradually become clear to you.

Your company has been bought by a conglomerate and they don't need two marketing departments. And, sure enough, your boss calls the whole department in one Monday morning and gives you the bad news—everyone is out.

But the most heartbreaking scenario is played out when you're called into your boss' office late on a Friday afternoon to be told that you're no longer welcome at Mega Corp. You will be replaced by someone with "more relevant experience" and thank you very much for your fifteen years of dedicated service. And your outplacement counselor is waiting in the next office to listen to you in case you feel like "venting"—which to some means crying; to others a spewing forth of anger and frustration at the inequity of it all.

Being fired is one of the truly unpleasant experiences of adult life. As we mentioned earlier, women do seem to take it harder than men—but an unlooked-for-termination is depressing and shocking for both men and women.

Even if you are not an employee who identifies strongly with your corporation or institution, you feel unwanted, unworthy, and insecure—your feelings are hurt.

We discussed your predictable depression and what you can do to alleviate it in Chapter III, but for now we want to make some other suggestions. It is important for your peace of mind and your future to negotiate as favorable a severance package as you can—and, believe it or not, it makes good sense for your company, as well.

Because so many people are being fired by our major corporations during this era of downsizing and reorganization, you may find your corporation to be surprisingly sympathetic to your plight. You may also find that you are in a reasonably strong bargaining position.

The last thing that any responsible corporation wants is a phalanx of displaced, vocal executives out in the marketplace looking for jobs and talking about how Mega Corp. chews up its executives and then spits them out to fend for themselves. Companies want you to leave in as contented a frame of mind as is possible under the circumstances. After all:

1. They have their reputations to consider. No corporation wants to become notorious for being an uncaring employer. It's amazing how quickly word gets out—if it does, they can forget about recruiting those bright new managers at reasonable cost.

2. Even corporations can feel guilty.   It's not easy for a traditionally paternalistic organization to turn its back on a faithful employee of many years. Even if necessity dictates the cutbacks, it doesn't mean that management is indifferent to the human condition of those who are being terminated. We've found that some corporations give extra consideration to those older employees who have been with the company for a long time.

It's true that blind loyalty to the corporation is fading fast—it's tough to remain enthusiastic about a company that has just let your friends go after fifteen years. But the absence of a dedicated, involved work force is bad news for a company—and they know it. But in many cases the need to cut costs is so great that they have, after corporate consideration, chosen what seems at the moment to be the lesser of two evils.

3. If there are too many disgruntled employees on the job-hunt trail who have been let go by one corporation, that company can become known as a "revolving door."   There would be no point in going to work for such a place because you wouldn't last six months. This may not be true at all, but bad reputations are hard to overcome, and become, ultimately, very expensive for management.

And it is quite serious for a major company to have trouble recruiting the best and brightest of both new and experienced managerial talent.

It is always unfortunate when a major corporation feels compelled to fire prominent executives—those who are well-known to the media and throughout the industry. It is just smart business, if the top-rung executives do have to go, to make the parting as friendly as possible. These top guns have access to too many influential ears—all of which can be translated into the most appalling publicity for Mega Corp.

4. Although a great many executives have been fired, obviously many remain.   It is extremely demoralizing for the corporate survivors to see friends and colleagues leave unwillingly, even if they are reasonably certain that their jobs are safe. Managers left behind become depressed and discontented. That's obviously no way to run a railroad or anything else.

It is good for both employees and corporation if the severed executives seem to leave with some interim support—a decent severance package, for example. Good employees want to work for a company that pays at least a modicum of attention to the real concerns of the people whom it employs.

5. *For the employer, the most pressing reason to have decent severance policies is legal.* In our increasingly litigious society displaced employees think nothing of bringing their employers into court claiming all kinds of discrimination: they were fired because they were a minority; they were fired because they were *not* a minority— reverse discrimination; they were fired because they were too old, too set in their ways, too close to retirement. A court case is expensive and nonproductive and employers want to avoid them whenever possible.

Many court cases have been settled in favor of the employee, so corporations have to be quite certain that they can prove that the terminated manager was let go for "just cause." Recent court decisions have found against the notion of "employment at will"—as in the good old days, when an employer could fire a manager simply because he didn't like him—and companies have found it more sensible to see that the fired employee leaves in a reasonably happy frame of mind or they will all end up in court.

Now, assuming that the corporate ax is about to fall on you and your job, you need to get yourself in shape for what will come.

Before you discuss a severance package in any detail with your company, be sure to talk with your accountant. Yes, that's right, your accountant, not your lawyer. You will want to know the best way to set up severance payments and how you can avoid paying too much in taxes. At this stage, you may not know exactly what you'll be offered, but at least you'll know how to manage it once a deal is made.

As you spend your weekend pulling yourself together, it might be a good idea to try to find out what the company has been offering in severance to others who have already left. Is there a previously terminated friend whom you could call? Don't pry, but if you know of someone who might not mind sharing information, remember that knowledge is power.

Most companies do offer some kind of severance deal. Swain & Swain conducted an in-depth survey of 100 large corporations asking them about their severance practices—particularly as they depart from stated policies. Ninety-one percent said that they offered severance pay, either as a lump sum or continuation of salary for a varying number of months, and 94 percent will allow the executive the use of an office and secretarial support for a specified time. Seventy-six percent made some sort of outplacement counseling available.

Treat the upcoming negotiations very much as a business; think of taking care of yourself as best you can until you can find another job.

Don't forget the concept of win-win negotiating. You want to come away with everything you think you're entitled to, but you don't want the company negotiator to feel as if he or she is being steamrollered or threatened.

Make a list of the points you want to cover. You may not be able to negotiate your way to success on each item, but every eight-year-old knows that "it doesn't hurt to ask."

What's on your shopping list?

1. Severance pay. If you have been with the company for a while and are at an executive level, you will obviously get more than short-term employees in the lower ranks. Some companies have a formula that ranges from a low of one week of pay for every year of service to far more generous packages. Check with your accountant, but it will probably be better for you to receive the severance pay on a monthly basis—not in a lump payment, primarily because medical benefits will usually be paid for by the company only if the person is still considered "on continued salary." We have noticed that fired employees who have been given more than six months' pay have a tendency to lag through the job search process. They are complacent; but remember that even a generous settlement will run out—and it takes time to find the right job, which is the purpose of the severance pay.

2. Continuation of health benefits. As we mentioned in an earlier chapter, it is almost impossible to duplicate the sort of coverage that you enjoyed with group insurance. If, of course, you become a midpreneur, you will have to make other arrangements, but for now insist that your medical-insurance benefits are continued.

3. Use of an office and secretarial aid. Many companies provide this for a limited amount of time for executives. However, outplacement firms can also provide this service.

4. Use of the company car if you have had one up to now. It is pointless for you to have to buy or lease a car if you may be offered one at your next job. It is, however, unlikely that this perk will be continued in today's more stringent separation packages.

5. If your accountant didn't think of it, don't forget to request compensation

if you've lost a pension. This should be added on to your negotiated severance pay.

6. Did you relocate because the company that you were working for wanted you in a job elsewhere? And then you were terminated? Help in returning to home base is not an unreasonable request. Being left in an unfamiliar place will likely add to the difficulty of your job search—and ultimately to "poor press" for your company.

   If you think that you would prefer being back in the city from which you moved, and that you would have a better chance at finding a job there, then by all means ask the company to move you back. In our severance-practices survey, 59 percent said that they would consider relocating the displaced employee again at the company's expense.

7. Ask for outplacement. It's the "perk" of the 1980s. We do realize that some readers of this book may not have the opportunity to make use of an outplacement firm—you may have been working for a company that is in a part of the country where an excellent firm is not readily available. But you should at least know what we do in case you are ever offered outplacement as an option.

Before we're accused of simply advertising in our own self-interest, we must point out that we fervently believe that outplacement firms can make the difference between getting a position of your choosing, or merely a job.

John Feldkamp is executive director of Brown & Wood, a law firm that offers outplacement to anyone who has been employed by them for more than two years.

"In cases of involuntary separation," says Feldkamp, "outplacement can make the circumstances much easier. It can take what could be a tragic situation and turn it into a positive experience."

And a corporate human resources executive agrees. Robert B. Mintz, Director of Management Resources at Time Inc., has told us that "at its best, I have seen outplacement be an incredibly liberating experience for people. For many, it is the first time to obtain objective feedback and to test hypotheses with an objective career coach. Done well, the assessment portion of outplacement helps the individual to put things in perspective and learn enough about themselves to avoid the traps of the employment market."

What is it exactly that corporate outplacement firms do?

Corporate outplacement firms work with individuals who are sponsored by their organizations. The sponsors engage the outplacement firm and pay the entire fee for the outplaced employee, who becomes the "client" or "candidate."

At Swain & Swain our philosophy is based on self-actualization and self-motivation. The best job-search efforts are self-initiated and self-sustained. We can help you with your job search; but only one person can actually *do* it—you. In this proactive approach, we will help you to recognize and capitalize on your strengths (while acknowledging realistic weaknesses) and position yourself for the kind of job that meets short- and long-range needs—your needs and objectives. We provide advice, counsel, confidentiality, objectivity—and a lot of reality perception.

In addition, we provide a place from which to conduct your job search.

We expect you to arrive in proper business attire. We don't want to see you in shorts and sandals—that does not reinforce the mood of businesslike dedication to the task of calling everyone you know who might contribute to the successful conduct of a job search.

At Swain & Swain, as well as at most of the other reputable outplacement firms, we offer a variety of services.

- Counseling. We have career counselors and psychological counselors on staff. You will meet with them and you will be helped in sorting through the directions in which your job search should proceed. If you feel that you need individual psychological sessions, psychotherapists are available to you.

- Testing. We administer vocational and psychological assessments. This is the time for you to consider a new career choice if you want to. Our assessments seek to establish where your significant interests, values, and abilities lie.

- Videotaping. We videotape mock interviews with you in a role-playing situation. These are extremely valuable and can make a positive difference in subsequent interview behavior.

   One of our young woman clients was turned down by a very dynamic company after the last in a series of interviews. We noticed in talking with her that she sprawled back in her chair, her arm draped over the back. "Was that the way you were sitting in the interview?" she was asked. Pause while she thought about it: "Yes . . . I guess it was." Us: "And what reason did they give you for your unsuitability for their company?" "That I might be a little too laid back for them," was her reply.

It turned out that our client was quite nervous during the interview and thought that her casual posture would indicate an ease that she did not feel. It backfired, but she did learn to sit in the approved, time-tested way: straight in the chair, feet on the floor, leaning slightly forward with attentive interest.

· Job-campaign counseling. We discuss strategies, and specific leads, and plan a schedule. We also help develop the résumé, and various kinds of cover letters that should accompany it.

· Office space and telephones.

· Reference library. We have the current business directories and other reference books to search out companies and key decision makers and their backgrounds.

· Secretarial and message service.

Finding a new job is a job in itself and involves many complexities—strategic and creative thinking. We have been called (affectionately): coach; mentor; guru; business adviser; strategist; tactician; sounding board. And as several appreciative people have expressed to us: "You always keep the ball moving!"

There are some companies—only a large corporation could afford to do it—who have set up their own company-run outplacement services: large banks, for example, have had internal departments since the mid-seventies. According to a survey of Fortune 500 companies reported on in the *United States Banker* of August 1986, 80 percent of the large corporations offered outplacement counseling of some kind to terminated employees—that's up from 40 percent ten years before.

After you have made your best deal with your old company be prepared to have the company ask something—perhaps several somethings—of you. This is acceptable and very much within the guidelines of win-win negotiating.

You may have been in a position to know company secrets: industries like the cat food manufacturers are extremely competitive and it is not a nice thought that you are out there in the marketplace with all the information about their latest line of cat crunchies in your head. Be prepared to sign an agreement that will prevent you from working for a competitor for a specified, but limited, amount of time. You may also find that once you have left you will not be welcome on the premises. The corporation does not want you in the halls, greeting old friends and colleagues, and picking up tips as to what's new in cat food.

Also be prepared to sign an agreement that you will not at some future date decide to sue your ex-employer for some real or imagined slight. Don't be offended—according to our severance-practices survey, a growing percentage of respondents ask their departing employees to sign such an agreement as a matter of course.

To sum up our advice: In order to protect your reputation as a reasonable adult—after all, the ex-employer of today may be tomorrow's purchaser of your free-lance services—accept the inevitable, do not throw tantrums, and exit as gracefully as possible.

But do bargain as well as you can before you are actually off the premises. Your employer may feel guilty—and *should* accept some responsibility for you—so make as favorable a deal for yourself as possible. Remember, it's in their best interest, too, in the long run.

Negotiating Your Way into the Corporation

Ideally, we hope that little time passes between your negotiations to leave a company and your negotiations to join one.

The negotiating technique is the same: you want the best possible deal for yourself without causing the corporation to think that you're a bad sort—demanding things that they hadn't even thought of.

Win-win negotiating is especially important with a new company. Some job hunters don't seem to understand that you can be too forceful a negotiator and don't know when to stop when they're making their deal.

One individual we have heard of—-a man who has always worked for financial institutions—has been fired four times in the last six years.

Apparently, he is always amazed that he keeps losing his job, but we think part of the issue is that he simply negotiates too well. He gets the jobs because he's well qualified, and seems to have the knack of laying the interviewer's doubts to rest. So they make him an offer.

But he bargains for benefits and perks and salary too well; he's too tough. When he's through with his demands, he's usually gotten what he wants, but the interviewer is a little resentful. And, more than likely, he can't possibly be as good as he's convinced them he's going to be. Nobody could be. So when he doesn't live up to his own advance billing, he's fired—again.

So there are good, sound, self-protective reasons for using win-win techniques: you shouldn't seem greedy and overbearing. After all, you should also have some interest in your new company and the job therein—not just what money and stock options you can wrest from them.

But remember, too, to try to get what the market will cheerfully bear. You have, after all, been offered a job, so you have convinced the company that you can make money for them. They want you, and you should be entitled to fair compensation.

Fair compensation is based on what you're worth to the company— today, tomorrow, and the day after that. If you've done your proper research, you have an idea of what similar employees on your managerial level are making and can expect to make. You may have been able to discover salary ranges, but projected increases may be harder to uncover.

Remember, too, that corporations feel they can no longer afford to be as generous with salary and benefits as they have been in the past. A great many programs—like supplying matching funds for a percentage of your salary if you put it in a savings or stock purchase plan—are being cut back or eliminated. Even in the largest corporations, the palmy days of corporate jets to monthly meetings are just about gone.

In your negotiations after the job offer has been made and you're thinking about accepting, the following categories should be explored by you:

1. Responsibilities. Clarify your responsibilities and the limits that may be imposed on your freely implementing them.

Do you have complete hiring and firing powers? Is it absolutely clear to whom you will be reporting? Do you have a budget, and how much of one? If there's a shakeup, what will it mean for you? Will you be able to renegotiate your position if your boss is changed? What are your chances for future promotion? Will you receive performance reviews at preordained intervals?

2. Salary. At this stage of the negotiation you have probably agreed to a salary to start. What remains is the opportunity to open the question of your salary increases as you go forward. But use your own judgment if you think that your new employer has already settled that question and is not open to further discussion about any salary dimension.

One vice-president of compensation and benefits, speaking at one of our monthly forums, suggested this sort of effort: your salary has been settled, but in the course of the negotiation you have been told that you will not be eligible for a bonus for six months. The vice-president suggested that you could, as you get up to go, say in an off-hand manner, "By the way, would you be willing to consider shortening the wait until I'm eligible for a bonus?"

Maybe they wouldn't be willing, but if you feel the climate is right, and you won't antagonize the interviewer, do ask.

3. Your insurance package. Most companies and all large corporations will offer life insurance and health benefits. But does the corporation pay 100 percent of the premiums? Today many organizations are no longer footing the bill. Do they have a decent dental plan?

Check out the health package. Does it cover your whole family and with a reasonable lifetime maximum payout?

What about disability insurance? Any plan ought to include long-term disability, which would generally be based on a percentage of your basic salary if it ever becomes necessary.

You may be very far from retirement but do ask about the company's plan for continuing insurance benefits after retirement. As of this writing, there is no real push for government-sponsored health insurance, so for the foreseeable future we will all have to look after ourselves. See if your plan can be converted into something worthwhile after retirement.

4. Cafeteria plans.   About 20 percent of all companies have these plans, which allow you to choose from a menu of different benefits. Although this benefit is mostly of interest to the younger middle managers, it can be very helpful to you especially if you have a spouse who also has a job with a corporation. You may, for example, be covered under her health and life insurance package and you could apply your own health insurance funds to a longer vacation or perhaps child care assistance. If your new employer does not have a cafeteria plan, and your old one did, see if perhaps you can set up your own similar package. Except for administrative costs, a tailor-made benefits package won't cost your new employer any more.

There are many specifics in your entering terms package that have to do with money. Among them are:

5. *Bonuses.* Sometimes it is financially advantageous from the company's perspective to give you what is in effect greater monetary compensation through a bonus system, rather than giving you the extra money as part of your salary.

There are several kinds of bonuses that may be offered.

You might receive a predetermined percentage of your base salary each year. For the middle tier it might amount to 40 to 80 percent, rising to as much as 100 percent for top executives.

Or the bonus might be based on company performance or perhaps the profitability of your own department. You will negotiate for the highest percentage possible.

And you might even receive a bonus on top of your bonus. This is given to help you pay the taxes that the additional income will generate. These extras would range normally between 30 and 35 percent of your yearly salary.

6. *Stock options or grants.* These are very popular and common benefits, but generally offered only to the upper stratum of managers.

Stock options came into vogue during the early fifties, as publicly or privately held corporations realized that the days of dedicated family management were gone.

If a manager owned shares in the company, they reasoned, surely he or she would have its best interest at heart. One could think of the plan as a sweetener to engender creative, profit-motivated management and company loyalty.

7. *Possibility of corporation-held loans.* These could be for college tuition for your kids, or a down-payment for a house. These loans are usually low-interest, and even if you never need one, it's comforting to know that it's an option.

8. *Pension plan.* How long will it take for you to become vested, and what happens if you leave the company before that time? Find out if you will receive any of the accrued funds along with your severance package.

The substance of your job is after all the main reason that you have accepted employment with this company, so examine the following categories and be sure that you can live with the company's policies.

9. Vacation policy.   Is corporate vacation policy generous or is this the kind of company where executives are expected to forswear time away from their desks for the good of the business? Your own lifestyle will decide for you if this is important. If you're a workaholic with an understanding spouse who can also never get away, while it may not be very good for your mental health it is your choice. You can accept the company policy.

10. Education benefits.   Will you be eligible for special training? An advanced degree, for example, or intensive executive training seminars. This may or may not be important in the field that you're in.

11. Relocation policy.   One of the most important things for you to know about if there is any chance that you might be relocated is what company policy is on this subject. If it is not generous, and you think that there is an excellent chance that you might be sent to another city, think about passing on this job opportunity. Especially if you have a family, it is vital that you receive company support if they expect you to uproot yourselves and deal not only with a new job but also all the problems that moving a household entails. You should be offered:

- Job placement help for your spouse. Many companies will aid your spouse in finding a job comparable to the one that he or she had to give up.

- Moving expenses. In some cases (as in the military), the company will take care of everything, from finding the movers to seeing that they arrive on time, to the packing of your household goods.

- Help with housing. This could include a variety of benefits ranging from the company supplying a house to finding a realtor to temporary housing until you find something suitable. The company may pay for one or more trips to house-hunt in the new area; interest-free loans if you have to buy a house before you've sold your old one; brokerage fees, mortgage points; legal fees; shipping of a second car—in general, although this ought not to be a money-making transaction, you should not be out-of-pocket because the corporation wants you someplace else.

- Also, be sure you spell out, preferably in writing, what will happen if you leave their employ nonvoluntarily, or what if you're unhappy in your work? Will you be stranded in a strange city? Ask the questions before you find yourself in that unpleasant situation. If you're being sent out of the country, make sure all the above points are covered in writing.

Make sure if you're going to be spending a few years in Europe, that the company gets you there and home in comfort. This is a situation in which you ought to insist on a contract.

There are countless miscellaneous benefits and perks that may be offered to you.

One oil executive told us of the beauty of the south Texas ranch that he would visit once a year to unwind. His company no longer can indulge in such largesse, but until the oil price slide they would lease the hunting rights to shoot deer and birds in one of the last unspoiled spots in this country. Our friend didn't happen to want to shoot anything, but he enjoyed the outdoor life and the change of pace.

More usual offerings include free tax advice, a company-paid car, membership dues for associations and country clubs, free travel for family members—a whole range of things that make life in your area of the country more pleasant.

Think about whatever perk is especially important to you in case there has to be a tradeoff. As long as your demands are reasonable and clearly not against the company's best interest, you should have no hesitancy in asking; they might say no, but they might also say yes.

Once you've worked out the details of your employment, get it in writing. Contracts are rare except at the very top, but a letter agreement can be binding. If the company does not think to summarize your agreement in writing, it's perfectly all right for you to write the letter enumerating your understanding of responsibilities and rewards as you see them.

Chapter X
The Midpreneurial Venture

Success (n.)—doing what you want to do and making money from it.—[anon.]

Are You a Mippie?

Are you a Mippie? Or could you be? In the Swain & Swain definition, a Mippie is an ex-corporate employee who has followed his or her heart to a goal that many of us have dreamed of—a business of one's own, with controlled risk.

"Mippie" is derived from our word "midpreneur," a coinage, we feel, whose time has come. The relationship to a buzzword of the eighties, "entrepreneur," is obvious, but the difference is profound for someone who has spent most of his or her working life in one or more paternalistic corporations.

We usually conjure up the image of bicycles at Swain & Swain to demonstrate the difference between an entrepreneur and a midpreneur. An entrepreneur is a risk-taker, totally and completely. He or she creates the business idea, develops it, brings it to fruition, and reaps the rewards—or suffers the losses. This is the unicycle rider—teetering sometimes on the brink of falling, but when successful enjoying an exhilarating ride.

Envision the midpreneur as a bicycle rider, too, but this person is mounted on a two-wheeler; also a risk-taker of sorts, but somewhat more cautious. The midpreneur, although stepping out from under the protective corporate canopy, will perhaps adapt an existing idea, or continue to expand a business found to be successful.

Key to midpreneur's operation is sharing the risk. This is a reactive individual, who looks about in the surrounding commercial milieu and sees an idea that can be modified, expanded, transformed in some way to their benefit.

A generation ago, potential members of this new midpreneurial class would have stayed safely ensconced in their jobs for life. If they were unlucky enough to lose them—which was quite rare unless they were unfit in some way—then they suffered humiliation and beat the bushes until something similar to the job they had left turned up.

We talked in Chapter I of the shrinking managerial class. It's clear what that means to terminated executives—there are fewer places for them to find new jobs.

Ten years ago, if one examined the goals of displaced managers, fewer than 5 percent would have been interested in trying a commercial venture of their own. Most moved to another corporation as soon as they could. But today, there's more to think about than just getting another job. Managers are becoming wary about putting their faith in any company—the company itself doesn't know what the future may be. No employee who has lived through a major corporate bloodbath is eager to repeat the experience.

With the new uncertain business environment, risk taking at least *seems* less terrifying. If you were to plot the likelihood of losing your job if you joined another company, or failing financially if, for example, you hung up your shingle as a consultant, you might not find the lines on the graph so far apart. And no matter what, the worst that would happen is that you'd be back in the job market. (We might as well say right here in the beginning of this chapter that the life of a midpreneur is not for you if it would mean mortgaging your house, selling your car, and putting your small children to work. The idea of a noncorporate venture is to expand your spirit, not to throw you into financial debt and emotional collapse.)

Some executives who find themselves about to be unemployed or already out the door have weighed the risks and found them acceptable—among the people whom we counsel, that group numbers over 20 percent of all our outplacement clients.

If the idea of *not* joining yet another corporate or institutional family strikes you as wildly exciting, how can you judge whether (a) you have a chance at success and (b) you will be happy?

At Swain & Swain, our clients take self-assessment tests, talk with psychologists and counselors, and do some serious thinking out loud—all in an attempt to understand their own personalities and real job-related desires, as well as more practical matters of seeing whether the commercial ventures that they have in mind will fly.

There is no reason why you—with the aid of your spouse or a friend or colleague who knows you well, and might even be interested in joining you in some sort of business venture—can't, on your own, at least try to figure out whether the life of a Mippie might be for you.

There are two basic elements to consider: you as a personality and your business idea.

Not everyone ought to swim in the midpreneurial waters. One of our clients who wanted to start his own small business tested very high in creativity, but on the very low end of the scale in the category of decision making. Conferences with our psychologist and a backup battery of tests simply underscored his indecisiveness. We advised him to return to the more structured environment of a corporation, which he eventually did. Was it a mistake for him not to try his lifelong dream? Not at this point in his development. Not being ready to act, even with controlled risk, strongly suggested the likelihood of losing his capital and confidence. Far better that he still has the vision of his own business—not an impossible idea, for instance, if down the road he meets a partner who can supplement the areas in which he's weak.

As you've probably gathered throughout this book, at Swain & Swain we try to guide our clients in developing more self-awareness. You are the only person who can decide what you really want; you are the only person who can decide if the path that seems interesting is one that is practical for you; and you are the only one who can make success happen.

There are no sureties in predicting whether someone is going to be successful in a midpreneurial or entrepreneurial venture.

But certainties or not, as you go through your soul searching and decision making, you should try to assess what sort of personality you have, what tasks make you feel more or less comfortable. There is no question that certain personal and physical characteristics, as well as a very broad spectrum of work-related abilities, although not a guarantee of success, will make a midpreneurial attempt easier for you if you have them.

At the beginning of this chapter we asked if you *could* be a Mippie. You will be able to answer that question better after you contemplate the list of traits below. You don't need to have them all in order to be successful on your own, but you should be able to recognize more than 50 percent as part of your own personality and management style if you're even going to think about midpreneurialism.

1. Do you like to take risks? This is obviously vital—it doesn't mean the Las Vegas or commodities market type of risk, but rather not knowing what your income might be in a few years. Can you live with no financial guarantees? Realize that you may not know exactly what your income will be from one week to the next. If not knowing what level you will have reached in six months is going to drive you crazy, then your personality is not suited to the life of a midpreneur. There are lots of companies and other institutions out there; one of them could use your services.

2. Are you a self-starter and can you get the work out, even if your office is your kitchen table? You may be one of those people who absolutely needs the structure of the nine-to-five day imposed by the corporation.

3. Do you enjoy hard work and are you energetic? If you're over forty-five and aren't what you once were on the tennis court, don't worry. If you find the idea of trying your own venture exhilarating, that will see you through as long as there are no serious health problems.

If you do have some health problems—a mild heart condition, for example, or any other slightly debilitating problem, this certainly does not remove you from midpreneurial consideration. You would, however, have to think about your plan carefully and try to remove as many stressful issues as you can. Remember that part of the midpreneurial ethos is to share the risk. You could ally yourself with a going management consulting firm, for example, and do occasional work for them. This would eliminate the strain of starting up and finding new business, and you might find a situation in which you could work as many hours as you wanted to.

4. Do you have self-confidence? If you're going to have to depend on yourself for your livelihood, clearly you must have faith in yourself and your abilities to handle frustration and adversity. Will you be at ease in presenting your service or product to strangers when you're not too sure of your reception?

5. Do you have a history of getting to the bottom of things? Do you take initiative if a problem arises, and do you rely on yourself for solutions?

6. Do you like people?   Do you have trouble managing employees? Are you either autocratic or too indecisive? Any difficulty that you might have had with interpersonal relationships in an office setting is going to be much worse if you have staff in your new enterprise because you are now the BOSS, and any venture is obviously going to be much more important to you than it is to your employees. If you've had trouble with staff in the past, try to develop empathy. It is extremely important if you're running your own enterprise to try to figure out how the other fellow feels—whether it's an employee, potential client, supplier, spouse. If you are not intuitively empathetic, you can achieve much the same result by *listening* carefully to what people tell you.

7. Are you trustworthy?   Were you brought up to believe that your word is your bond? There are many strata in American business in which a more Machiavellian culture prevails. But if you've pulled some fast ones in the past, better rethink your ethics. There may be lots of sharp dealing on a grand scale, but when *you are* the company, with perhaps a partner, or just a few employees, you're going back in time to the days when a handshake was as good as a contract. You won't last six months if clients can't depend on you.

8. Are you a forceful decision-maker?   You will have to make quick decisions, and then live with the results.

9. Are you inordinately discouraged by failure?   Disappointment is natural, but paralyzing depression is not. Every mistake should be a learning experience, from which you emerge with a greater understanding of the pitfalls in your field.

10. Can you accept criticism?   The source may be a dissatisfied customer or client, your spouse, your accountant, your partner. If your previous job was not in a team situation—perhaps you were a high-level person who worked alone on new concepts—it may be difficult for you to understand what's required in the give-and-take of a group effort. If you think that you could not bear to engage in the confrontations that are bound to arise because they always do in business, then the midpreneurial route is not for you.

11. If you make a commitment, do you generally stick with it?   Were you the kind of child that actually finished making the model planes that came with about four thousand pieces? And have you retained those tenacious, steady qualities in adulthood? Can you be happy without instant gratification, but rather keep your eye on that far away carrot?

12. Do you need the trappings of a well-known organization to feel important?   If you call a client or a supplier as a representative of the Boeing Corporation, or the Ford Foundation, or Harvard University, you are going to get action. But, do you have the energy to achieve recognition on your own, by establishing your relationships with those clients and suppliers?

13. Do you believe that you control your own destiny, and that bad breaks are simply to be overcome?   Psychologists call this the "internal locus of control," and it is the belief that allows you to take full credit for your own accomplishments, and stresses also that setbacks are simply the downside of being your own boss.

14. Are you well-organized?   This may be nothing more than making sure that your books are up-to-date each evening, but if you have a tendency to let paperwork pile up, and you will be in this venture alone, be prepared to hire someone to help. Even the simplest sort of free-lance service operation has to answer to the IRS—and they expect to see records.

15. Can you formulate and implement a business plan?   Also, as the midpreneur, you are the one who will have to formulate the business plan, and you are the one who will have to follow through. You will, of course, have the help of other professionals—lawyer, accountant, banker—to fill in the gaps in your own experience. But they are advisers only; if you are not an idea person, then you have little business even thinking about being a midpreneur. On the other hand, don't neglect the good offices of those whom you've hired to help. There are bound to be things you don't know. Recognize what areas these are—don't wing it.

16. Are you flexible?   It's important to have a plan and then implement it, but if you're to be a success, you cannot rigidly refuse to modify a plan when a better idea comes along.

Management consultant Wendell O. Metcalf sums up for us efficiently in a booklet published by the Small Business Administration. Metcalf isolates five broad categories of traits that show a significant statistical correlation with success:

- <u>drive</u>, which is composed of responsibility, vigor, initiative, persistence, and good health;

- <u>thinking ability</u>, encompassing original, creative, critical, and analytical thinking;

- <u>human relations ability</u>, which comprises emotional stability, sociability, cautiousness, personal relations, consideration, cheerfulness, cooperation, and tactfulness;

- <u>communications ability</u>, composed of verbal and writing skills;

  and (the area that is not covered in our list of sixteen personality traits)

- <u>technical knowledge</u>, all the information that you might have about the process of producing goods and services and your ability to apply this information in a practical way.

Obviously, without the technical knowledge you cannot succeed. You may have patted yourself on the back for having each of the sixteen traits—you might be well-organized, and flexible, and energetic, and so on—but if you have not educated yourself sufficiently in the details of your proposed venture, then you will assuredly not succeed.

So before you even *think* of having your business cards printed, see how many of the following you can answer with a firm yes.

1. Do you understand that time really is money, and you must learn not to give it away?   Later in the chapter we will discuss a formula for pricing your services if you're a consultant, but it is important to put a value on your time no matter what business you've gone into— just as if you were still working for a large corporation. You are still the same skilled professional that you were while on the payroll. Many people who work out of their homes in service businesses complain that they are not taken seriously by friends who cannot seem to understand that while it *is* their own business, if they spend all their time on the phone chatting, they're not billing clients!

2. Once you have decided what your midpreneurial venture will be, do you think that you will have utter confidence in it?   When you sell to either a client or buyer, you must be wholly enthusiastic. If you are lukewarm, you cannot expect anyone to be interested in you or your product.

3. Are you skilled enough in your new field to assess the potential need for your product or service adequately?   All the enthusiasm in the world is not going to make a successful venture out of a flower shop that sets up in a rural area where most people have elaborate gardens. But raise some horses on those fields where you were growing zinnias and dahlias, and you might get a good trade going in horse manure. Expand into a garden center, with rakes and peat moss and garden hoses, and you have a shot at success.

4. Do you have a "name" in your field? If your midpreneurial venture is in a field allied to the one in which you have recently been employed—you're going to try consulting, for example—what expertise and skills do you bring with you? Do you have many contacts in the industry? Do you have a viable network of colleagues who will recommend you for jobs? Do you have an excellent reputation in your field? Have you been active in an industry-wide organization and is your name well known in your field?

5. How is your salesmanship? Are you persuasive? Have you, while in a corporate situation, gotten your ideas and projects adopted and implemented?

6. Do you have, or can you get, enough money? Not only do you need capital for your venture, but you must have enough in the bank for you and your family to live on in case expected income doesn't materialize.

7. Are you used to being in charge? In any midpreneurial venture, you will have to be responsible for the implementation of your service, or the delivery of your product, from inception to completion. You will probably not have much staff to take care of details. You'll have to do it yourself.

You're going to have to pay for stamps, and health insurance, and taxis. The expense account stops now. No more salary-matching program, or bonuses. There are a lot of items that are vital to the running of the business. You will have to pay for them, so when you budget try to think of every necessary supply and service that you might have used in an average day at the office.

8. Where will you work? From your home? If this is your plan, be very wary. If you must set up your office at home for financial or convenience reasons, be sure that you set aside a place that is only for business. Be there at the start of the work day, dressed for the office. This does not necessarily mean a tie and jacket or silk dress if you're going to spend the day at your desk making phone calls, but it doesn't mean pajamas or shorts either. Don't get caught up in a second cup of coffee at the kitchen table or a long conversation with your child's first-grade teacher or the afternoon soaps. If you have an office at home, keep office hours.

It's your money that you're spending now, but don't save it in ways that are going to doom you to failure. There are some ventures that cry out for style. If you can't do them right, it's better not to bother with them at all, as it's absolutely predetermined that you will lose your investment. In interior design, for example, you have to look successful just to attract business. If all you can afford as office space is a loft in an unfashionable warehouse district, forget it. By the time the neighborhood becomes chic, you'll be out of business.

9. How well do you actually know the field that interests you? Are you taking on too much? More than you ought to at your level of expertise? For example, if you understand the manufacturing end of whatever item it is that you're offering, have you ever worked in sales or advertising? If you're a production person, what about the financial end? You may be doing nothing more complicated than making apple butter, but you'd better understand the operation from the buying of the jars through the amount of sugar to use through the printing of labels through the distribution to gourmet shops. If you know how to do all that, you're unusual, because not too many Renaissance people come out of the corporate world. But if you *don't* understand all the hidden corners in each of these processes, you ought to hire someone who does. This is not necessarily a permanent hire—there are plenty of free-lance consultants available. Hire another midpreneur.

10. Have you established your own free-lance network? *Before* you drum up business, you'd better be sure that you have a card file of professionals to call on if you get overbooked. You don't want to turn down work, but you can't miss deadlines, so you may reach the point at which you will need temporary help. Nothing could be easier if you've searched out these people beforehand.

Do We Really Need Another Chocolate Chip Cookie?

We've talked about our definition of midpreneurial: the key aspect is that the Mippie takes a controlled risk; this is an exercise in adapting, not creating. The midpreneur tries to refine and expand an existing idea, and ideally works with a product or service he or she knows something about.

It is fashionable for the media to call the eighties "the decade of the entrepreneur." The shrinking corporate pyramid is not just an artist's sketch in a magazine article. As a class, middle managers, although not an endangered species, are going to become rare birds. We may be on the threshold of a new era of self-reliance and creativity as each year another generation of potential managers leaves our colleges and tries to find a place in the work force.

Television, magazines, and the newspapers thrive on human interest stories about entrepreneurial geniuses. We've all read about brilliant refugees who, after seemingly learning English in a week, figure out the techniques of success in Silicon Valley and, pooling all the hard-earned resources of their extended family, invent a needed high-tech item and in six months are listed on the American Stock Exchange.

This is an exaggeration, but in the last few years remarkable success stories are being lived by a great many foreign entrepreneurs in the United States. Cubans, Asians, Russian Jews—these are all ambitious groups, many members of which came to this country with good educations. Some were fortunate enough to leave their country of origin with their families and money or salable goods, but if their emigration was due to the conditions of war, like the Cambodians, they came with very little, but discovered communities of their own countrymen who were already established and could help.

This book is not a survey of the business situation in this country—our main purpose is to try to indicate to the reader where new opportunities might lie—but we mention these new groups of immigrants because they are good examples of both the entrepreneurial and midpreneurial spirit. Between the creative business efforts of those new to our country and those who are leaving the structure of the corporations, the ranks of the self-employed are ballooning. As time goes on and the numbers grow these people will become a powerful economic force in the United States.

When a popular magazine describes a new and successful commercial enterprise, we would usually categorize it as entrepreneurially driven—with all the earmarks of high risk, interesting creativity, original conception. But occasionally we see a good example of true midpreneurialism.

A recent issue of *New York* magazine, which covers the New York City scene from every conceivable angle, published an article about the problems of starting a new business in its namesake city. Although most of the examples in the article had involved the very high risks of entrepreneurialism, we found the story of Ellen Fine, who had spent years in the upholstery business and knew her materials and what clients wanted. Ellen was working at Bloomingdale's when it occurred to her that it was very hard to find really first-rate fabrics in retail stores. Anything that was very special had to be ordered. Building on that idea, she designed a pushcart—not an enormous outlay of funds—and, positioning herself at the South Street Seaport, a renovated part of the waterfront and a tourist attraction in downtown New York, she sold from her cart articles like pillows and sweaters that were made of the wonderful fabrics that she had been unable to find in the stores. Buyers liked her products, and she now has two retail stores in New York as well as five in other cities. This midpreneur took a limited risk, worked at something that she understood well, and was successful.

Our favorite Swain & Swain success story is about a client who has become something of a local and national celebrity: locally, because he's become a media event in his hometown of Ridgefield, Connecticut; nationally, because his story piqued the interest of the *Wall Street Journal*, which told it to its readers in December of 1986.

Michael Soetbeer is a former personnel director for a New York City hospital, in his early fifties now, who was let go when hospital management changed. When Michael came to us for outplacement, we found it hard to find any area of consuming interest that he would be comfortable in pursuing.

As he talked with his counselor, he became elated when he discussed his vacation adventures in the Caribbean—he and a friend chartered a sailing vessel and sold shares to passengers to meet expenses. Michael's friend did the skippering and navigation,

Michael was the quartermaster and cook, and enjoyed every minute of it.

It was very easy for us to figure out what Michael shouldn't do, but an idea for the perfect new career was harder to come by. In excellent midpreneurial style, Michael's wife, Jane, came into the picture. One guideline of the midpreneurial venture is to take on an already successful operation—if one understands its quirks and difficulties.

Jane found an ad in the local paper, placed there by a retired lawyer who had established a French-style hot dog stand that he had set up in the main street of Ridgefield. Further investigation showed that the stand was doing well, but the lawyer's wife was not pleased that her distinguished husband was now a food vendor, for the entire town to see. Ridgefield, Connecticut, is *very* upscale.

But the Soetbeers had no such qualms, and so Michael bought the business and improved on it until it is now arguably the fanciest hot dog stand in the country. Called Chez Lenard, the stand offers Perrier and lime to wash down the exotically prepared hot dogs, which sell for $4.95, and upon which you can have a fondue topping made of cheese, white wine, and cherry brandy.

Michael Soetbeer loves his new work, is planning to franchise the idea in Florida, and is making more money than ever before. And Ridgefield loves him. Chez Lenard is the only portable food stand permitted and apparently stores on the main street compete to have Michael set up shop in front of their doors. And, Michael says, "I only take orders from my customers today."

What are the elements that go into successful midpreneurial venture?

The standard advice given to apprentice writers, particularly those who are attempting fiction, is: "Write about what you know." This is also excellent advice for the midpreneur. Equally important as the need to share risk is the bottom-line necessity to know what you're doing in every area, or if you're new to the venture, to have the guidance of a person or organization who can help you understand your goals, develop your idea, and implement your marketing plan, even if what you're marketing is yourself.

Some basic guidelines that apply to almost every venture:

Concentrate on a field that you know well, and one that interests you—or, better yet, one that fascinates you. We find that a great many of our clients often try to turn a hobby into a commercial venture. This is an excellent idea, but you can run the risk that spending too much time with something that used to provide a pleasurable break, particularly now that the stakes are high, may ruin the pastime for you.

Gardening and cooking are two hobbies that people who have left the corporate world often turn to when they go into business for themselves. These midpreneurs may start a small catering business, or become landscaping consultants. There is a good chance of success if the business is in the right sort of affluent area and the new midpreneurs really are good at their erstwhile hobbies.

The sorts of hobbies that can be turned into small businesses are as varied as people's interests: sewing, weaving, pottery, crafts of all kinds; an interest and expertise in the outdoors could lead to a company that supplied guides as well as trained clients in outdoor skills; thorough knowledge of a popular foreign country could enable the midpreneur to arrange unusual tours, perhaps led by a cooking expert, or an art historian or archaeologist.

Many midpreneurial enterprises, which by definition start in a self-contained, manageable way, use the knowledge that the employee has gained in the industry that he or she has just left. They become free-lancers or consultants, sometimes hired by the very company that has let them go. These days it's a truism that although corporations may not be willing to "buy" employees, they are interested in being able to "rent" them, if for no other reason than someone has to do the work previously done by the terminated middle managers. Even though the corporations may be paying rather stiff consultants' fees, it is very often financially prudent to do so—for example, the company might not need the free-lancer or consultant year-round, perhaps just during the busy winter season. And, of course, they then avoid being saddled with those expensive costs that come under the heading of "benefits package"—insurance, bonuses, Social Security tax.

Buying a franchise is another possibility. If you do your research, you can establish which companies are reputable, which already have the good will of the public, and which will honor their commitment to train you properly. Or you may buy a small neighborhood business that has been successful for years and furnishes a necessary product or service to the area. Warning: Look into the lease very carefully. In some cities, this is just the sort of business that a landlord wants out—

to make room for something much more upscale, usually part of an expensive chain or a shop with an international reputation; in other words, a business that is willing to pay inflated rents and is able to do so.

Some of the towns in the Hamptons out on New York State's Long Island are sorry examples of this. With wildly uncontrolled development has come the rich condo-dweller who demands that the local stores stock the *Wall Street Journal* and cold take-out shrimp-and-pasta salad. Gone are the charming little crafts shops, or local grocers, or even the farmers' markets. They had to make room for gourmet delis and expensive clothing boutiques. Be sure you don't find yourself in such a situation—if you buy a local business, make certain that the area is stable.

Do you have the "people support" that you will need?   Whether this is a spouse to help you with the books, or a stable of available freelancers to help you out if need be, as well as your professionals—lawyer, accountant, banker—have everyone lined up before you begin doing business.

Money.   This is one area in which you need the help of an accountant before you find your first job. Do you have savings? Will you be borrowing from friends and family? Will you have to borrow from financial institutions? If you have to go to commercial lenders, be sure you understand all the terms, whether you've approached a bank, finance company, credit union, savings and loan; don't sign anything until your accountant or lawyer has seen it.

Another caution. A venture of one's own is an excellent solution for some of our clients, and they end up being more successful than they ever were working for a corporation.

But the Small Business Administration has estimated that although about half a million new businesses are started each year, about the same number bite the dust. The reasons? Poor management due to inexperience and misuse of capital.

You have your idea, but you cannot get started in its implementation until your marketing plan is in place.   You have to know how to position your product or service, how to market it, or yourself if you're the product; how to figure costs, profits, how much to charge for your time.

We give the same advice to all our clients who decide that they would like to try a midpreneurial project, and we would like you to pay attention to this suggestion too: even though you think you understand your idea, and you've gone over the costs again and again, and you have handsome new business cards and boxes of letterhead, before you commit any of your time to this endeavor, and before you spend any substantial amount of money, *call in the professionals.*

Your Professional Team

You will need at the very least the experience of an accountant and a lawyer. *These should not be close friends or members of your family.* This is a business relationship and you should pay them. If you're using your brother-in-law to file for incorporation, for example, it may take too long and you will have a terrible family fight and you will never talk to your sister again. Isn't it easier to keep it on a cash-and-carry basis?

Think of your accountant and lawyer as technical consultants whose advice you heed. Obviously, you trust these people or you would not have chosen them. If either one was the result of a recommendation, make sure that you trust the judgment of the person who did the recommending, and that they are enthusiastic about the professionals' skills. Choose your accountant and attorney with the same care that you would a surgeon, especially if your forte is not in the financial or legal areas. You are trusting part of your future to these people.

What sort of advice might you expect from each, and in what areas should they advise you?

THE LAWYER: If your venture is rather modest and uncomplicated—if, for example, you and a colleague are going to look for work in management consulting—then you will not need extensive help from your lawyer at this stage. If you will be marketing a product, then you might need a little more attention. But, basically, once you've given yourself the go-ahead, all you have to decide now that requires legal advice is what form your business should take. You have three choices: (1) single proprietorship, which is the simplest form of business, but would leave you unprotected in case of a liability; (2) partnership, which has certain restrictions but is inexpensive to set up and might provide some tax advantages; it also leaves you vulnerable to lawsuits; or (3) incorporation, which is the most expensive to set up, the most closely regulated by the government, and often leads to double taxation for the partners; the main advantage is that you are subject to only limited liability in case of legal difficulties.

It is not our intent in this book to teach you how to run a small business—we merely want you to understand what you should expect of the lawyer you hire. Clearly, you use him or her for all legal matters, which at this stage should not be many: to draw up a partnership if necessary, to file for incorporation, to check over any contract that you are asked to sign. If the lawyer indicates that you are too small potatoes to spend much time with, then find another one. There are plenty of attorneys about who are willing to grow along with your business, and you want someone who will be available to you when you need them.

THE ACCOUNTANT: This person will be your most important consultant, and, like your lawyer, you want someone who will spend time on your account, even though it's small right now. This is the person with whom you'll be in touch at least twice a month no matter how modest your cash flow at first. If success comes quickly, your accountant will be on a retainer and will handle complicated office matters—estimating taxes, helping you with bank loans, putting a value on inventory—all the hundreds of tasks that you will have to deal with if you sell a product or service and it catches on. In this case, your accountant will act as a business manager.

But at the very least, your accountant will:

- Help you decide what sort of business organization—partnerships or sole proprietorship—is best for you.

- Figure out your taxes, and see that you're in good repute with the IRS.

- Help you with financial projections. Can you afford to expand? Should you put money back in the business?

- Figure out what your operating expenses will be each month and presumably help you to learn to compute these figures for yourself eventually.

- Set up your books and show you how to keep them.

- Aid you in learning to read financial statements.

· Work with you and a bank to set up your account or apply for a loan.

· Be a general financial and business adviser as you get started.

Your early relationship with the accountant is a training period. You want to work with someone who will explain *why* certain things are being done. By the end of the first year, you ought to be able to at least understand your tax returns, as well as be comfortable with your bookkeeping system. Your goal is to reach the point at which you could handle the financial end of your operation if you had to. After all, it's your business, and your financial papers should hold no mystery for you. The details of your business must be as accessible to you as they are to your accountant.

It's your responsibility to see to it that you complete your business education. It may take further training, such as courses in accounting or management—the accountant ought to be able to advise you on what's most necessary and helpful. If your accountant is not helpful, get a new one.

In complicated matters of pricing a product, you will need financial advice until eventually you come up with a formula that appears to furnish you with a profit. In time, you will discover to your joy how accurately you calculated.

But what if you are a free-lancer, or a consultant, perhaps selling your services to the sorts of companies that used to employ you?

You know enough to keep careful records of all work-related expenses for your tax return, but you discover that when *you* are the product to be sold, you haven't any idea about what to charge.

We offer our clients two guidelines at Swain & Swain, and either method might very well furnish you with the same result.

1. Ask around the industry.   If you used consultants while still in corporate employ, then you know what you paid them. Even so, it's a good idea to call colleagues at other companies and try to find out what other rates may be.

You might have to be crafty, perhaps present your request under the guise of helping a friend. Or, if your colleague knows that you're now in business for yourself, suggest that a certain price (your best guess) was the amount charged *you* by a consultant that you used for a project. You want to know if the cost seems out of line. You may not fool anyone, but you'll probably at least get a reaction that the amount you suggested was much too high or ridiculously low.

2. Do this two-step calculation. We've asked around various industries, too, and the answers that we got enabled us to set up a simple formula. Our research also provided good news for the consultant who works alone. You're going to be cheaper than a consultant who comes from a large management consulting firm. The way they generally figure what they will bill the client is as follows:

A. Start with an employee's base salary, say $50,000 a year. Divide that by the 200 billable working days in the year. Then the large firm usually multiplies that figure by three, to make sure they get their profit and overhead. The client would be billed for $750 for a day's work.

B. To figure your charges as a consultant working on your own, you will follow the same formula, except that you will multiply the $50,000 divided by 200 by *two*. You would charge $500 a day, a large saving to the client. You don't have the overhead that the large firm has. Presuming you have good credentials, you could be a real bargain to the client.

If after weighing positives and negatives you decide to go the midpreneurial route, we wish you every success in your endeavor.

If you're persistent and ingenious, and your business goes well, you may agree with one of our clients who made the switch to midpreneur successfully: "All those years in an office I felt as if I was being stifled," she said. "This is like coming home."

Epilogue

We work each day with individuals who have one thing in common: each is in transition. Some are better prepared than others to forge ahead with a new job, a new idea, a new career. Only some volunteered for the "change." Many have not been content for some time with the direction or progress of their careers, while others had been seemingly satisfied—until someone else forced the decision, leaving them with no choice but to seek another opportunity.

Being in the center of so much change and transition, we have come to see it as a largely positive and productive time for most people. It is, however, apparent that many of us do not spring into action until we must, preferring to protect ourselves from the uncertainty of change and not heeding the warning signals—until it's too late. One clever fellow wryly observed, "The handwriting on the wall is not a forgery."

We hope the information we've provided has helped you in the process of initiating your career plans. Whether your desire is to mount a campaign to leave an unsatisfactory job, develop a workable plan for the future, or achieve a midpreneurial opportunity, we hope that the information between these covers has helped you in:

- Thinking through your current situation in a realistic, positive way;

- Assessing your own strengths, weaknesses, personal values and goals;

- Inspiring you to action—while removing some of the fears, anxieties and "mystique" surrounding another one of life's major changes.

We thought you might find further inspiration as you go about tailoring your own strategic plan in some additional stories of others before you who effected career changes—and who became far happier individuals as a result.

In reflecting on the case studies of those who achieve growth and success in the changes they made, it became evident that they all shared these characteristics as they went about planning and implementing their objectives:

- Perseverance;

- A realistic sense of themselves and how to achieve their objectives—with a sense of humor;

- Flexibility and open mindedness;

- A positive attitude.

Here are some vignettes of actual tales of personal change and growth.

A Change from Academia

John was the discontented headmaster of a private, girl's preparatory school in the northeast. At age 41, married with two children, he felt there was more to life than what he referred to as the "fishbowl" existence of being head "guru" to adoring students. He actually arranged his own outplacement, getting the trustees to agree to support him in a program to help him redirect his future at a crucial stage in his life and career.

Having achieved his desired goal to leave the academic world, John has found happiness as the partner in a consulting firm serving a client base of private schools throughout the country. He was able to apply his knowledge and experience within the academic world and his skill in advising and educating to a lucrative, personally satisfying career in specialty consulting.

Manager Changes Careers—from the Not-For-Profit to the Profit World

Beth had been a communications director of an educational institution and, having spent all of her career within the confines of higher education, at age 45 was feeling the necessity for change—both for financial and psychological reasons. When she was terminated from her position, due to a political battle that left her on the losing end, she resolved to achieve this goal.

After identifying potential areas for her expertise, Beth realized that an appropriate target for her was within the management consulting and financial services area. Her objective was met when she "created" and accepted the position of director of public relations and communications for a large, prestigious financial-services organization whose culture was similar to the one she left. Here she was able to bring her marketing and communications skills to an organization that had never developed this function, but recognized the absolute necessity at this competitive juncture in their industry.

Now five years and several promotions later, Beth is happy and prospering.

Manager Leaves Corporate Life Behind

Arthur, a 53 year-old vice-president and creative director had spent the last 25 years of his career with a major publishing company, working for several of their publications and enjoying periodic raises, promotions, and all the perks inherent in corporate life.

When he became a victim of a massive reorganization and lost his job, he spent the first few months looking for a similar position. Realizing his heart wasn't in it, he decided to explore the feasibility of establishing his own corporate communications business and leave the corporate world forever.

Starting as a "freelancer," Arthur is now heading his own growing firm, employing five people and serving Fortune 100 clients. From his perspective, life has never been better. He doesn't have to deal with corporate politics, is his own boss, can work his own hours, and has final say over the creative process.

Changing Industries Mid-Life

At age 49 Harriet was terminated from her position as director of marketing for a large consumer products company, after over 20 years with them. The company had recently been acquired and she and several others were found to be "redundant."

Her biggest concern was, having stayed so long at one company and having had a "flat" career there for the past six years, how would she be perceived by executive recruiters and the rest of the outside world? She felt that opportunities in her own field might be limited and she had run out of "steam," leading her to look outside her industry in her search.

Harriet's search led her to a senior marketing position with one of the nation's largest, most competitive banks. Her consumer-products marketing experience was seen as exactly what was needed in a time of deregulation and heavy emphasis on marketing—with few people on board to provide the solid, classical marketing background she had.

Having gone from the perception of being a "minor player" to an up-and-coming "woman to watch," she is flourishing and realizes that without her involuntary "push" to leave she'd never had reached her current position.

An Executive Leaves the Corporate World for a Professorship & Midpreneurial Career

Nigel, a 42 year old oil company executive with dual citizenship in the U.S. and the U.K., lost his footing on the corporate ladder in a major downsizing that affected his position as an ex-patriate living in London.

With his children already grown and his own interests leading him towards things intellectual and aesthetic, Nigel decided to make the switch from the corporate to academic world, where he is delighted to serve in his role of professor of international affairs at a medium sized college. The rest of his time is devoted to buying and selling antiques with his business partner, his wife.

He is finding his students far more receptive to his ideas than he felt senior management had been and feels he has fully integrated his personal values and tastes with his creative, intellectual, and ego needs.

A Controller Now Controlling the Finances of Rock Stars

George, a 38 year old corporate controller was phased out of his job when a new boss took over the finance department and decided that he and George were never going to see eye-to-eye on matters financial.

In exploring various options, the goal became that of "how to make an avocation into a vocation." His love was preparing tax returns and financial planning for some fledgling and up and coming musicians. With a sound business plan and sense of how to network and position himself within the entertainment world, George began to develop his clientele, offering financial and accounting services. They are happy that he understands their lifestyle and "eccentricities" and he has forged a new, fulfilling career for himself.

Thinking about our own personal business lives, neither of us would be doing what we are, which we find highly satisfying, had it not been for a combination of circumstances that at the time appeared to be less than auspicious, e.g., dissatisfaction with a current job, involuntary termination for one of us, and the need for greater earning power, autonomy, and control over our own destinies.

While change is one of the hardest things for human beings to accept—let alone embrace—it is through change that all of us grow, expand our horizons, enrich our environment, and ultimately achieve fulfillment. There's no question that "enforced" change such as the loss of a job can be highly stressful and anxiety producing.

But, when we examine the alternative, it would appear that we have but one choice: to become an "opportunist" in life's continuously changing scenarios, seizing the moment for the chance to turn misfortune, mismatches, misconceptions, and missed expectations into your own success.

As another wit once said referring to life in general, "As far as I know, this isn't a dress rehearsal." So, reader, let's go for it!

Later, when you have arrived at a new, desired career destination, please write to us and share your experience. We look forward to hearing from you. We wish you all the best in making your desires become reality.

MADELEINE AND BOB SWAIN
% *MasterMedia Limited*
215 Park Avenue South
Suite 1601
New York, NY 10003

Appendix A

Outplacement International

Cambridge Human Resource Group
2 North Riverside Plaza/Suite 2200
Chicago, IL 60606-2703
(312) 454–9009

F. Craig Barber
Calhoun Square/Hennepin & Lake
Minneapolis, MN 55408
(612) 374–3200

Fitzgerald, Stevens & Ford, Inc.
747 Main Street/Suite 126
Concord, MA 01742
(617) 369–0455

Mulford Moreland & Associates, Inc.
20300 Stevens Creek Boulevard/Suite 320
Cupertino, CA 95014–2217
(408) 446–2966

Nelson Harper & Associates
2408 East Biltmore Circle Suite C220
Phoenix, AZ 85016
(602) 996–0906

New Options Group, Inc.
Redwood Tower
217 East Redwood Street/Suite 1970
Baltimore, MD 21202
(301) 576–8390

PMG/Denver
6000 East Evans Avenue
Building Two, Suite 400
Denver, CO 80222
(303) 759–9313

Promark Company
Mariemont Executive Bldg.
3814 West Street
Cincinnati, OH 45227
(513) 561–1881

Reedie & Company
8235 Douglas Avenue
Suite 1111—Lockbox 56
Dallas, TX 75225
(214) 361–5678

RMA Consulting
2233 Huntington Drive
San Marino, CA 91108
(818) 795–4548

Seagate Associates, Inc.
Paramus Plaza/12 Route 17 North
Paramus, NJ 07652
(201) 368–1660

Swain & Swain, Inc.
The Chrysler Building
405 Lexington Avenue
New York, NY 10174
(212) 953–9100

The Transitions Management Group
444 Market Street/Suite 333
San Francisco, CA 94111
(415) 981–0202

International

Sanders & Sidney Plc.
9 Park Place, St. James's Street
London SW1A ILP
(01) 491–0491

Appendix B

An OPT Application

Charles, a forty-five-year-old middle manager, lost his job in a planned reduction-in-force that was handled well by his company. He completed the OPT Forecast below to see how long it should take him to find another position. *The Situation.* The company's separation support was fair, leaving no hidden agendas. Charles isn't interested in switching careers, has no reason to relocate, and will be conducting his search in the fall and winter seasons. Result: Subtract four weeks.

But the following situational factors add twelve weeks to Charles' search: only fair proximity to target jobs; a child in special school, limiting the range of his search; a poorly developed network; and a salary below "fast-track" levels (i.e., two to three times his age).

Net: Add eight weeks.

Style and Attitude. Charles has a highly acceptable management style, good work habits, pleasant interpersonal skills, and reasonable expectations. In addition, he operates as a team player, tolerates frustration well, and remains optimistic under stress. These factors subtract sixteen weeks.

On the other hand, Charles could be more decisive, show more energy, exude more confidence, and display greater sophistication. These negatives add four weeks to the forecast.

Net: Subtract twelve weeks.

Job Search Abilities. Nothing but added time here. Charles' ability to focus, prioritize, "manage up," sell himself, write clearly, listen effectively, negotiate, and follow through are mediocre at best.

Net: Add thirteen weeks.

Health and Appearance.   For Charles, this category nearly is a wash. His good health is counterbalanced by some off-putting mannerisms and a thoroughly unremarkable appearance.

Net: Add two weeks.

Career history.   Again, more added time. Charles has spent his career with a so-so company in a mature industry. At present, there is little demand for his expertise and experience.

   On the positive side, Charles' career has shown stability. He has been in his last position for enough time to prove that he's not flaky, but also has experience with more than one company.

Net: Add four weeks.

Family, Age, and Education.   In this final category, Charles' status added time. He is married, but his wife doesn't work. His age is also seen as a slight negative.

Net: Add two weeks.

Summary.   As noted, Charles has a favorable "Style and Attitude" (-12 weeks), but this advantage is wiped out by the unfavorable counts of the other categories ($+29$).

The forecast: A job search of seventeen weeks.

Charles' Chart
Your Situation . . . Conditions and Circumstances of the Moment

Factors

* If you have been terminated, how traumatic has it been for you?

* Do you harbor a "hidden agenda" (i.e., revenge, "I'll show them")?

* Do you have access to "networks" and are you willing to use them?

* Do you intend to make a career change?

Realistically, how much time do you have to find another position?

Will there be a relocation involved?

How close are you to your targeted job marketplace?

Do any circumstances limit your job-search flexibility?

†If you are an expatriate, how long have you been away?

What time of the year is it?

Are you in a minority group (i.e., black, Hispanic, female)?

		SOMEWHAT	VERY MUCH
	◯	+2	+4
		POSSIBLY	YES
	◯	+3	+6
	YES	MAYBE	NO
	−4	+1	(+5)
		MAYBE	YES
	◯	+3	+4
	REASONABLE	NOT ENOUGH	CONSIDERABLE
	(−2)	+3	+6
		MAYBE	YES
	◯	+3	+4
	CLOSE	SO-SO	NOT CLOSE
	−3	(+1)	+5
		SOME	SIGNIFICANT
		(+2)	+6
	UNDER 5 YEARS	5 TO 9 YEARS	OVER 10 YEARS
	+1	+3	+5
	FALL-WINTER	SPRING	SUMMER
	(−2)	−1	+3
			YES
	◯		+4

*Indicates variable factor
†Not applicable

Your Situation . . .

Factors

Will you be perceived as a "fast-tracker" (i.e., salary and title progression)?

	YES	POSSIBLY	NO
	−3	−1	(+4)

Your estimates . . .

−4	+3	+9

Your Style and Attitude

Factors

* How decisive are you about choices and direction?

VERY	MODERATELY	NOT VERY
−3	(+2)	+4

* How do you think your confidence will be throughout a job search?

HIGH	MIXED	LOW
−4	(+2)	+4

* How well do you tolerate frustration?

	SO-SO	NOT WELL
( )	+1	+4

* How much are you affected by stress?

	SOMEWHAT	VERY MUCH
( )	+1	+4

* What is your general outlook on life and work?

OPTIMISTIC	MIXED	PESSIMISTIC
(−3)	+1	+3

* Are you concerned about your age?

	SOMEWHAT	VERY MUCH
( )	+2	+5

	DEMOCRATI- CALLY	TO FIT THE MOMENT	AUTOCRATICALLY
How do you manage your jobs and others?	(−4)	+2	+5
		SOMETIMES	RARELY
Do your work habits exceed nine-to-five limits?	( )	+1	+3
	GREGARIOUS	PLEASANT	SHY
How would you describe your outward manner?	−4	(−3)	+6
	MOSTLY	SOMETIMES	RARELY
Do you see yourself as a team player and do others agree?	(−3)	+1	+4
	AN OPPORTUNITY	MIXED	HAS TO BE PERFECT
How do you view a job search at this point?	(−3)	+2	+5

Your estimates . . .	−13	+1	

*Indicates variable factor

Your Abilities . . . As They Relate to a Job Search

Factors

* How well do you focus and prioritize?

* How well do you follow through?

* How are you in one-on-one situations and communications?

* How are you in stand-up presentations?

* How is writing for you?

* Are you a good listener?

* How often do you read "signals"?

* How comfortable are you with negotiations?

VERY WELL	MIXED	WITH DIFFICULTY
−2	(+2)	+5

VERY WELL	MIXED	WITH DIFFICULTY
−3	(+2)	+5

VERY COMFORT-ABLE	MIXED	UNCOMFORTABLE
−3	(+1)	+3

VERY COMFORT-ABLE	MIXED	UNCOMFORTABLE
−4	(+2)	+4

EASY	MIXED	DIFFICULT
−2	(+1)	+3

ALWAYS	SOMETIMES	SELDOM
−4	(+2)	+5

ALWAYS	SOMETIMES	SELDOM
−2	(+1)	+5

ALWAYS	SOMETIMES	SELDOM
−3	(+2)	+4

Your estimates . . .

	+13	

*Indicates variable factor

Your Career History

Factors	4 TO 8 YEARS	UNDER 1 YEAR	OVER 20 YEARS
How long have you been with your present employer?	(−2)	+2	+4
	3 TO 5 YEARS		OVER 8 YEARS
How long have you been in your present position?	−2	◯	+3
	2 OR 3	OVER 5	ONLY 1
How many companies have you worked for?	(−2)	+3	+4
	GROWING	MATURED	SHRINKING
What is the condition of your present industry?	−3	(+1)	+4
	GOOD	FAIR	POOR
What is the recent performance of your employer?	−2	(+1)	+3
	ADVANCING	FLAT	DECLINING
How will the outside world view your career path?	−3	(+2)	+3
	HIGH	MODERATE	LOW
What sort of demand exists for your experience?	−4	+1	(+4)
		MODERATELY	PROBABLY NOT
Are you considered current in your field?		(−1)	+3
	LINE	BOTH	STAFF
Will you be seen as a "line" or "staff" person?	−3	(+1)	+3

Your estimates . . .	−4	+4	+4

Your Health and Appearance

Factors

	EXCELLENT	FAIR	NOT SO GOOD
* What is your present physical well-being?	(−3)	+1	+5
		SOMETIMES	FREQUENTLY
* Do you have an "issue" with alcohol or drugs?	( )	+6	+12
		SOMETIMES	FREQUENTLY
* Do you exhibit any nervous mannerisms?		+2	(+4)
	EXCELLENT	ORDINARY	NOT GOOD
* What is the state of your "public" wardrobe?	−2	(+1)	+4
	TRIM		HEAVY
* What is your weight?	(−2)		+3
		SOME	CONSIDERABLE
Have you experienced any ill health in the past five years?	( )	+2	+4
	ATTRACTIVE	ORDINARY	PROBLEMATIC
How do you rate your physical appearance?	−3	(+1)	+4
	TALL	AVERAGE	SHORT
What is your height?	−2	(+1)	+2

Your estimates . . .	−5	+3	+4

*Indicates variable factor

Your Family Status, Age, and Educational Background

Factors	FULLY	MODERATELY	NOT VERY
*How supportive will your spouse be in a job search?	−3	(+2)	+4
	YES	SOMETIMES	NO
Does your spouse work?	−2	+1	(+3)
	MARRIED	DIVORCED	SINGLE
What is your marital status?	(−1)	+2	+4
	45 TO 54	55 TO 59	OVER 60
Are you a member of the following age groups?	(+2)	+3	+6
	FULLY	SO-SO	NO
Does your education match your career goals?	(−2)	+2	+4
	YES		NO
Did you attend a top school?	(−2)		+2
Your estimates . . .	−3	+2	+3

*Indicates variable factor

OPT Forecast—Total Estimates

Transfer the totals of the −'s and +'s from each category to the boxes below:

Category

	−'s	+'s	
Your Situation	−4	+3	+9
Your Style and Attitude	−13	+1	
Your (Job-seeking) Abilities		+13	
Your Career History	−4	+4	+4
Your Health and Appearance	−5	+3	+4
Your Family Status, Age, and Educational Background	−3	+2	+3

−'s	+'s
−29	+46

NET ESTIMATE

+17

Suggested Reading

Additional Reading

Allen, Louis L. *Starting and Succeeding in Your Own Small Business*. New York: Grosset & Dunlap.

Bern, Paula. *How to Work for a Woman Boss—When You'd Rather Not*. New York: Dodd, Mead & Company, 1987.

Berne, Eric. *What Do You Say after You Say Hello?* New York: Bantam Books, 1975.

Birsner, E. Patricia. *Job Hunting for the Forty Plus Executive: A Handbook for Middle-Aged Managers and Professionals*. New York: Facts on File Publications, 1985.

Blanchard, Kenneth, and Spencer Johnson. *The One Minute Manager*. New York: Berkeley Books, 1986.

Bolles, Richard N. *The Three Boxes of Life: And How to Get Out of Them*. Berkeley, California: Ten Speed Press, 1981.

————. *What Color Is Your Parachute? A Practical Manual for Job-Hunters and Career-Changers*. Berkeley, California: Ten Speed Press, 1987 (updated annually).

Bostwick, Burdette E. *Ill Proven Techniques and Strategies for Getting the Job Interview*. New York: John Wiley & Sons, 1981.

Brandon, Nathaniel. *How to Raise Your Self-Esteem*. New York: Bantam Books, 1987.

Byrne, John A. *The Headhunters*. New York: Macmillan, 1986.

Deal, Terrence E., and Allan A. Kennedy. *Corporate Cultures*. Reading, Massachusetts: Addison-Wesley, 1982.

231

Djeddah, Eli. *Moving Up*. Berkeley, California: Ten Speed Press, 1975.

DeRoche, Frederick W., and Mary A. McDougall. *Now It's Your Move: A Guide for the Outplaced Employee*. Englewood Cliffs, New Jersey: Prentice-Hall, 1984.

Ellis, Albert. *Anger: How to Live with and without It*. Secaucus, New Jersey: Citadel Press, 1977.

Fleming, Charles. *Executive Pursuit: The Insider's Guide to Finding Super Jobs Through Headhunters*. New York: New American Library, 1984.

Gelles-Cole, Sandi, ed. *Letitia Baldrige's Complete Guide to Executive Manners*. New York: Rawson Associates, 1985.

Hennig, Margaret, and Anne Jardim. *The Managerial Woman*. Garden City, New York: Anchor Press/Doubleday, 1977.

Holtz, Herman. *How to Succeed As an Independent Consultant*. New York: John Wiley & Sons, 1983.

Howell, Barbara. *Don't Bother to Come In on Monday: What to Do When You Lose Your Job*. New York: St. Martin's Press, 1973.

Jackson, Tom and Davidyne Mayleas. *The Hidden Job Market for the Eighties*. New York: Times Books, 1981.

Kennedy, Marilyn Moats. *Office Politics*. New York: Warner Books, 1981.

La Bier, Douglas. *Modern Madness: The Emotional Fallout of Success*. Reading, Massachusetts: Addison-Wesley, 1986.

Lipman, Burton E. *The Professional Job Search Program: How to Market Yourself*. New York: John Wiley & Sons, 1985.

Margerison, Charles. *How to Assess Your Managerial Style*. New York: AMACOM, 1979.

McCaslin, Barbara S., and Patricia P. McNamara. *Be Your Own Boss: A Women's Guide to Planning & Running Her Own Business*. Edgewood Cliffs, New Jersey: Prentice-Hall, 1980.

McCormack, Mark H. *What They Don't Teach You at Harvard Business School*. New York: Bantam Books, 1985.

Metcalf, Wendell O. *Starting and Managing a Small Business of Your Own*. 3rd ed. Vol. 1. of The Starting and Managing Series. Washington, D.C.: Small Business Administration, 1973.

Molloy, John T. *Dress for Success*. New York: Warner Books, 1975.

————. *The Woman's Dress for Success Book*. New York: Warner Books, 1978.

Montgomery, Robert L. *Listening Made Easy*. New York: AMACOM, 1981.

Nierenberg, Gerard I., and Henry H. Calero. *How to Read a Person Like a Book: And What to Do about It*. New York: Cornerstone Library, 1972.

Perry, Robert H. *How to Answer a Headhunter's Call: A Complete Guide to Executive Search*. New York: American Management Associations, 1985.

Peskin, Dean B. *Sacked! What to Do When You Lose Your Job*. New York: AMACOM, 1979.

Petras, Ross, and Kathryn Petras. *Inside Track: How to Get Into and Succeed in America's Prestige Companies.* New York: Vintage Books, 1985.

Pettus, Theodore. *One on One: Win the Interview, Win the Job.* New York: Random House, 1981.

Richardson, Jerry, and Joel Margulis. *The Magic of Rapport: The Business of Negotiation.* New York: Avon Books, 1985.

Scott, Robert. *How to Set Up and Operate Your Office at Home.* New York: Charles Scribner's Sons, 1985.

Staff of Catalyst. *What to Do with the Rest of Your Life.* New York: Simon & Schuster, 1980.

Szykitka, Walter, ed. *How to Be Your Own Boss.* New York: New American Library, 1978.

Timmons, Jeffry A., Leonard E. Smollen and Alexander L.M. Dingee, Jr. *New Venture Creation: A Guide to Small Business Development.* Homewood, Illinois: Richard D. Irwin, 1977.

Warschaw, Tessa Albert. *Winning by Negotiation.* New York: McGraw-Hill Book Company, 1980.

Wegmann, Robert. *Looking for Work in the New Economy.* Salt Lake City, Utah: Olympus Publishing, 1985.

Welch, Mary Scott. *Networking: The Great New Way for Women to Get Ahead.* New York: Harcourt Brace Jovanovich, 1980.

Wood, Orrin, G., Jr. *Your Hidden Assets: The Key to Getting Executive Jobs.* Homewood, Illinois: Dow Jones-Irwin, 1982.

Wright, John W. *The American Almanac of Jobs and Salaries.* New York: Avon Books, 1982.

Zate, Martin John. *Knock 'em Dead.* Boston: Bob Adams, Inc., 1985.

Zilbergeld, Bernie. *The Shrinking of American Myths of Psychological Change.* Boston: Little, Brown & Company, 1983.

Directories

Directories are basic sourcebooks. They may contain names of companies, their executive rosters, addresses, phone numbers, financial information, product or corporate service descriptions—hundreds of facts that will help you as you plan your job-search campaign.

Your local libraries—university, school, institutional, public, specialized—are the places to find directories. Investigate the business shelves carefully—you may uncover treasures that are full of detailed information about your city or region. Two examples found by us, for example, in a nearby library were the *Directory of Connecticut Manufacturers* and the membership directory of the *Long Island Association of Commerce and Industry*—either one just packed with new possibilities.

Below we have listed some of the standards that you might expect to find in a well-stocked business section or business library.

To begin with, look for any directory published by the following four organizations. Many are updated annually, and they cover most of the manufacturing and service companies in the United States.

Dun & Bradstreet, Parsippany, New Jersey:

Million Dollar Directory. Lists top 50,000 industrial corporations; includes names of executives.

Principal International Businesses. The 50,000 leading enterprises in 133 countries.

Reference Book of Corporate Management. Lists major corporations and personal backgrounds of management.

Moody's Investors Service, New York, New York:

Handbooks and manuals include alphabetical and geographical listings of national and international public companies, and statistical and financial data on those corporations. Some titles: *Bank and Finance Manual, Handbook of Common Stocks, Industrial Manual, Public Utility Manual, Transportation Manual.*

National Register Publishing Company, Wilmette, Illinois:

Directory of Corporate Affiliations. Detailed view of more than 4,000 corporations and their divisions, subsidiaries, and affiliates.

International Directory of Corporate Affiliations. In-depth listing of non-U.S. holdings of U.S. parent companies, as well as international holdings of foreign enterprises.

Macmillan Directory of Leading Private Companies. Corporate structure, assets, management information, financial data of 2,000 of the largest private parent companies in the United States.

Standard Directory of Advertisers. Lists more than 17,000 advertiser corporations and their annual advertising appropriations.

Standard Directory of Advertising Agencies. Lists agencies, with key personnel, accounts, billings.

Standard's & Poor's Corporation, New York, New York:

Corporation Description. This semi-monthly publication gives corporate background, stock data, and earnings.

Register of Corporations, Directors, and Executives. 3 vols. Guide to 45,000 corporations; includes addresses, phone numbers, officers, amount of sales, number of employees, personal information about executives.

In Addition

Consultants and Consulting Organizations. Janice McLean, ed. 6th ed. Detroit, Michigan: Gale Research Company, 1986.

Corporate Finance Sourcebook. New York, New York 10019. Lists firms that provide financial services. Annual.

Directory of Executive Recruiters. Fitzwilliam, New Hampshire: Consultants News, published annually.

Directory of Management Consultants. 4th ed. Fitzwilliam, New Hampshire: Consultants News, 1986.

Directory of Outplacement Firms. 4th ed. Fitzwilliam, New Hampshire: Consultants News, 1986.

Directory of Top Computer Executives. Phoenix, Arizona: Applied Computer Research, published semiannually.

Foundation Directory. 10th ed. New York: The Foundation Center, 1985.

Franchise Opportunities Handbook. Andrew Kostecka, comp. Washington, D.C.: U.S. Government Printing Office, 1985.

Green Book. New York: American Marketing Association, published annually. International Directory of Marketing Research House and Services.

Law and Business Directory of Corporate Counsel. Clifton, New Jersey: Law and Business. Annual reference to the organization and personnel of the nation's corporate legal departments.

Literary Market Place. New York: R.R. Bowker Company, published annually. Directory of American Book Publishing, with names and phone numbers of executives.

Securities Industry Yearbook. Barbara Van Dyk, ed. New York: Securities Industry Association, published annually. Ranking of firms based on capital; overview of the securities industry.

Index

About the Authors

ROBERT SWAIN

Bob Swain, Chairman of Swain & Swain, spent a number of years in organizational consulting and outplacement counseling prior to forming his own firm. He began his career in time-study work in a plant environment for a Fortune 500 company and was an early participant in the introduction of computers to corporate operations and reporting. Promoted to planning and marketing positions, he gained insight into the successful interaction of planning, operations, marketing, and finance prior to becoming an organizational consultant. Since founding the firm, Bob has advanced the development of innovative job-search programs, based in part on original research into key issues that bear on hiring decisions. He has written numerous articles on "Job-Search Marketing" and is quoted frequently on the subject of corporate and management changes and trends in *The Wall Street Journal*, *The New York Times*, and other publications.

MADELEINE SWAIN

Madeleine Swain is President and Chief Marketing Officer of Swain & Swain. Prior to participating in the formation of the firm, she headed her own marketing services company with clients in publishing, consulting, financial services, and informational products. Previously, she held positions in marketing, communications, graphic design, and advertising firms. As an outplacement consultant (and one of the few women principals in the field), Madeleine has been quoted widely in the business press and has authored articles on issues impacting career mobility. Madeleine is listed in *Who's Who in American Women* and is a founding member of the Association of Outplacement Consulting Firms and Outplacement International, a capitalized partnership of outplacement firms in the United States, Europe, England, and Canada.

Additional copies of *Out the Organization* may be ordered by sending a check for $11.95 to:

MasterMedia Limited
215 Park Avenue South
Suite 1601
New York, NY 10003
(212) 260-5600

MADELEINE AND ROBERT SWAIN are available for keynotes, half-day, and full-day seminars and workshops. Please contact MasterMedia for availability and fee arrangements.

Other MasterMedia Books:

The Pregnancy and Motherhood Diary: *Planning the First Year of Your Second Career,* by Susan Schiffer Stautberg, is the first and only undated appointment diary that shows how to manage pregnancy and career. ($12.95 paper).

Cities of Opportunity: *Finding the Best Place to Work, Live and Prosper in the 1990's and Beyond,* by Dr. John Tepper Marlin, explores the job and living options for the next decade and into the next century. This consumer guide and handbook, written by one of the world's experts on cities, selects and features 46 American cities and metropolitan areas. ($12.95 paper and $24.95 cloth).

The Dollars and Sense of Divorce, by Dr. Judith Briles, is the first book to combine practical tips on overcoming the legal hurdles and planning finances before, during, and after divorce. ($10.95 paper).

Aging Parents and You: *A Complete Handbook to Help You Help Your Elders Maintain a Productive, Healthy, and Independent Life,* by Eugenia Anderson-Ellis and Marsha Dryan, is a complete guide to providing care to aging relatives. It gives practical advice and resources to the adults who are helping their elders lead productive and independent lives. ($9.95 paper).

Criticism in Your Life: *How to Give It, How to Take It, How to Make It Work for You,* by Dr. Deborah Bright, offers practical advice, in an upbeat, readable, and realistic fashion, for turning criticism into control. Charts and diagrams guide the reader into managing criticism from bosses, spouses, relationships, children, friends, neighbors, and inlaws. ($17.95 cloth).

Beyond Success: *How Volunteer Service Can Help You Begin Making a Life Instead of Just a Living,* by John F. Reynolds III and Eleanor Raynolds CBE, is a unique how-to book targeted to business and professional people considering volunteer work, senior citizens who wish to fill leisure time meaningfully, and students trying out various career options. The book is filled with interviews with celebrities, CEOs, and average citizens who talk about the benefits of service work. ($19.95 cloth).

Managing It All: *Time-Saving Ideas for Career, Family, Relationships, and Self,* by Beverly Benz Treuille and Susan Schiffer Stautberg, is written for women who are juggling careers and families. Over 200 career women (ranging from a TV anchorwoman to an investment banker) were interviewed. The book contains many humorous anecdotes on saving time and improving the quality of life for self and family. ($9.95 paper).

Real Life 101: *(Almost) Surviving Your First Year out of College,* by Susan Kleinman, is a light-hearted guide to making the transition from campus to career. It offers the new graduate solid information on work, money, housing, health, and even finding happiness. ($9.95 paper).